M000301488

Contents

//

Foreword

///

The purpose of the Rules of the Road is to save lives and prevent injury on our roads. The rules apply to all road users: drivers, pedestrians, motorcyclists, horse riders, cyclists and those in charge of animals.

The rules ask us to take personal responsibility for our use of the road, and in doing so become better, safer and more socially responsible road users.

The Rules of the Road book is designed in an easy-to-read format and is written in plain English. It is your responsibility to read the rules and know them. At the back of the book, there is a Glossary that explains some of the terms we use. The rules are also published in Irish.

The rules comply with and reflect the Road Traffic Law as at 1 March 2015. Where planned changes in the law are known with certainty, a comment is included in the appropriate section to ensure the content reflects the changes. It is important to check the relevant section of the Road Safety Authority web site www.rsa.ie for updates.

We can save lives and prevent injury by changing our behaviour. Reading these rules and applying them will help achieve this goal.

It's our responsibility.

It's our choice.

Introduction

//

The rules of the road are for all road users – drivers, pedestrians, motorcyclists, horse riders, cyclists and those in charge of animals – for example, dog walkers. You must have a satisfactory knowledge of these rules to get a driving licence. Learning about road safety doesn't stop once you pass a driving test. It is an ongoing process.

You need to update your skills and knowledge and be aware of changes to road traffic laws. This is why you should understand and obey these rules whether you are learning to drive or have been driving for many years.

This book uses a 'how to' approach and covers many of the manoeuvres identified as factors in a road crash. It uses three methods to set out clearly and concisely how the law applies to all road users.

- It uses must and must not to draw attention to behaviour the law clearly demands or forbids.

- It uses terms such as **should** and **should not** to tell you how best to act in a situation where no legal rule is in place.

- It illustrates and describes traffic lights, road markings and the signs used to regulate traffic.

You play a vital role in preventing a crash. Knowing the rules of the road, practising good driving skills and taking care as a road user will make road safety policies more effective.

The more effective the policies, the greater the positive impact on you and your family's life, as well as the lives of others.

For example, a 5km/h difference in your speed could be the difference between life and death for a vulnerable road user such as a pedestrian. Research shows that when:

- hit by a car at 60km/h, 9 out of 10 pedestrians will be killed;

- hit by a car at 50km/h, 5 out of 10 pedestrians will be killed;

- hit by a car at 30km/h, 1 out of 10 pedestrians will be killed.

Source RoSPA UK

To guide you when on the road, there are a number of skills expected of all road users, drivers in particular. Drivers are expected to have:

- the ability to act responsibly;

- the ability to foresee and react to hazards;

- good concentration; and

- a good level of driving expertise.

As a road user, you are also expected to have a positive and considerate attitude to other road users, and, in particular, to vulnerable road users such as cyclists, motorcyclists, pedestrians, children, people with disabilities and older people.

In the interest of road safety, you need to be aware of the importance of gaining a good knowledge of this book and putting that knowledge into practice.

The overall aim of this book is to promote safety, good driving practice and courtesy in using our roads according to the law. It is an interpretation of the law from a road safety point of view; it is not the law. If you have a query, you should check the original legislation or ask a Garda.

The booklet covers the road traffic laws currently in force, but it will be updated regularly to take account of new laws.

It is worth noting that a failure on your part to obey the Rules Of The Road does not automatically mean you will be prosecuted, but if you are involved in a civil or criminal court case, your failure to obey the rules may be considered when deciding whether or not you are liable.

In the last 50 years the law on the use of the road has evolved and changed, and it continues to do so. At its most basic, the law on the use of the road protects road users, and it does so by virtue of three basic rules.

You **should**:

- always be able to stop within a distance you can see to be clear. You need to be able to control the vehicle you are driving to the extent that you can stop without causing a problem for anyone else on the roadway. The rule means you must be alert and exercise due care and attention at all times.

- always take the prevailing road conditions into account. This is common sense and means you must take account of any factors that will have an impact on your ability to drive safely and securely on the road. For example, the weather, the type of road, the condition of the road, the time of day, the type of the lighting;

○ always drive taking other users of the road into account. You need to take account of all of the things that can change on any given journey. For example, the volume of traffic and the speed of the traffic. Are there pedestrians, cyclists, animals? What are they doing? You cannot predict what others will do, and you shouldn't assume that you have priority. You need to make full allowance for all other users on the road.

You can choose to ignore the basic rules, but you do so at your peril. Ignoring the rules may create a dangerous situation which puts you and your passengers and other road users at risk. It may result in you breaking the criminal law and being prosecuted. If you are involved in a civil claim, a judge can hold you responsible.

It is in your interest to follow the basic principles of road safety when on the road.

Observing these three basic rules will help to keep you, your family, friends and other road users safe.

If you do not obey road traffic law, you could face a fine, penalty points and/or a conviction in court.

You might also be disqualified from driving and, in some cases, have to serve a prison term.

The road safety policies and laws in the country will work with the support of all road users.

REMEMBER

Driving is a life skill that requires your complete attention and lifelong learning to help you stay safe.

For up to date information, visit *www.rsa.ie*.

Section 1:

Driving licences and categories of vehicles

You **must** hold a current driving licence or a learner permit before driving any motor vehicle in a public place. You can drive only the type of vehicle for which you hold a licence or learner permit. And you **must** carry your driving licence or learner permit with you at all times when driving.

This section describes when and how to apply for or renew a driving licence. It also describes the different categories of vehicle to which the licences apply.

Categories of vehicles and minimum age for a first learner permit

The following table outlines the types of vehicle you may drive under each category of licence or permit, and the age you **must** reach before applying for a first learner permit in the relevant category.

Categories of Vehicles/Minimum Age of Driver/Restrictions

	Licence Category	Description of category since 19 January 2013	Minimum Age
	AM	Mopeds.	16 years
	A1	Motorcycles with an engine capacity not exceeding 125 cubic centimetres, with a power rating not exceeding 11 kW and with a power to weight ratio not exceeding 0.1 kW/kg. Motor tricycles with a power rating not exceeding 15 kW.	16 years
	A2	Motorcycles with a power rating not exceeding 35 kW, with a power to weight ratio not exceeding 0.2 kW/kg and not derived from a vehicle of more than double its power.	18 years

Licence Category	Description of category since 19 January 2013	Minimun Age
A	Motorcycles Motor tricycles	24 years or 20 with progressive access (see page 38). Persons under 21 years of age are not eligible to ride a motor tricycle.
B	Vehicles (other than motorcycles, mopeds, work vehicles or land tractors) having a Maximum Authorised Mass (MAM) not exceeding 3,500kg, having passenger accommodation for not more than 8 persons and where the MAM weight of the trailer is not greater than 750kg, or where the combined design gross vehicle weight of the towing vehicle and the trailer does not exceed 3,500kg. Quadricycles (other than those covered by category AM) are also covered by this category.	17 years
BE	Combination of drawing vehicles in category B and trailer where the MAM of the trailer is not greater than 3,500kg.	17 years
W	Work vehicles and land tractors	16 years
C	Vehicles other than those in categories D1 or D, or work vehicles or land tractors, whose MAM is over 3,500kg and which are designed and constructed to carry not more than 8 passengers in addition to the driver; motor vehicles in this category may be combined with a trailer having a MAM which does not exceed 750kg.	21 years or 18 with a Certificate of Professional Competency (CPC)
CE	Combination of drawing vehicles in category C and trailer where the MAM of the trailer is greater than 750kg.	21 years or 18 with CPC

	Licence Category	Description of category since 19 January 2013	Minimun Age
	C1	Vehicles other than those in categories D1 or D, or work vehicles or land tractors, the MAM of which exceeds 3,500kg but does not exceed 7,500kg and which are designed and constructed to carry not more than 8 passengers in addition to the driver; motor vehicles in this category may be combined with a trailer having a MAM not exceeding 750kg.	18 years
	C1E	Combination of drawing vehicles in category C1 and trailer where the MAM of the trailer is greater than 750kg and where the MAM of the drawing vehicle and trailer combined does not exceed 12,000kg. Combination of drawing vehicles in category B with trailer where the MAM of the trailer is greater than 3,500kg and where the MAM of the drawing vehicle and trailer combined does not exceed 12,000kg.	18 years
	D	Vehicles having passenger accommodation for more than 8 persons and where the MAM of the trailer is not greater than 750kg.	24 years or 21 years with CPC
	DE	Combination of drawing vehicles in category D and trailer where the MAM of the trailer is greater than 750kg.	24 years or 21 years with CPC
	D1	Vehicles designed and constructed to carry not more than 16 passengers in addition to the driver and with a maximum length not exceeding 8 metres; motor vehicles in this category may be combined with a trailer having a MAM not exceeding 750kg.	21 years
	D1E	Combination of drawing vehicles in category D1 and trailer where the MAM of the trailer is not greater than 750kg.	21 years

For further information on CPC, please see page 15.

If you are under 16 years of age, you must not use any vehicle in a public place.

Design Gross Vehicle Weight (DGVW) is the term used by manufacturers for the weight of the vehicle together with the maximum load it is designed to carry (including passengers, fuel, cargo and attachments). The DGVW is usually shown on a metal plate attached to the vehicle by the manufacturer. The DGVW may also be referred to as the Maximum Authorised Mass (MAM).

You must know and understand the carrying capacity of your vehicle or you are at serious risk of having a crash or causing harm. Overloading will reduce your ability to control your vehicle and is an offence.

Conditions attached to categories

Motorcycles

Holders of a driving licence for Category A are entitled to drive motorcycles with an engine output of any size.

Holders of a driving licence in category A2 are entitled to drive a motorcycle with an engine output of 35Kw or less, and a power to weight ratio not exceeding 0.20W/kg.

Trailers

Cars and trailers

If you hold a full category B licence, you may tow a trailer only if:

- the total maximum authorised mass (MAM) of the trailer is 750kg or less; or

- the combined MAM of the vehicle and trailer is no more than 3,500kg.

When you use a car to tow a heavier trailer, you must hold a category BE licence. A driver with a car/small van/4x4 and trailer licence category BE can draw a trailer where the MAM of the vehicle and trailer combination is greater than 3500kg but less than 7000kg.

Heavier vehicles and trailers

You must hold a Category CE, C1E, DE or D1E licence if you want to tow a heavier trailer. These are the licences that entitle you to drive the combinations of the towing vehicles and the trailer (see page 12). Equivalent licences issued before 19 January 2013 are EC, EC1, ED or ED1.

Heavy goods vehicles and buses

You must obey the law on tachographs. For full information please see *www. rsa.ie*.

Driver Certificate of Professional Competence (Driver CPC)

What is Driver CPC?

Driver CPC is a Certificate of Professional Competence for professional bus drivers (categories D1, D1E, D and DE) and professional truck drivers (categories C1, C1E, C and CE).

Equivalent licences issued before 19 January 2013 are D1, ED1, D, ED, C1, EC1, C and EC.

Driver CPC was introduced across the EU in 2008 for professional bus drivers and in 2009 for professional truck drivers. The three key aims are to:

- ensure that all professional drivers have good driving and safety standards and that those standards are maintained throughout their career;

- create a common standard for the training and testing of drivers throughout the EU; and

- reduce fatalities and serious injuries on Irish and European roads.

The Driver CPC and you

New Professional Driver

Since 30 September 2014 in order to become a professional bus or truck driver, you must take the following five steps:

- Step 1: Pass a driver theory test and obtain a driver theory test certificate for category C or D or both as appropriate;

- Step 2: Obtain a learner permit in the relevant category;

- Step 3: Pass a 2-hour case study theory test (note Step 2 must be completed before Step 3 if under 21 when applying for a C or CE licence or under 24 when applying for a D or DE licence);

- Step 4: Pass a 90-minute practical driving test, including questions and demonstrations on how you would carry out a series of checks; and

- Step 5: Pass a 30-minute practical test.

Once you have completed these steps, you must complete an application form (available from the RSA) to apply for your Driver CPC qualification card. The driving test (Step 3) and practical CPC tests (Step 4) are carried out at RSA driving test centres and are usually taken one after the other.

Further information about the Driver CPC programme is available on the RSA website, *www.rsa.ie*. Information about the Driver CPC Theory Tests is available on the following website: *www.theorytest.ie*.

Already a Professional Driver

If you were already a professional bus driver/holder of category D licence on 10 September 2008 or a professional truck driver/holder of a Category C licence on 10 September 2009, you are automatically entitled to Driver CPC. This is called 'acquired rights'.

In order that professional drivers maintain their rights they must complete 35 hours of periodic refresher training every five years.

Where a professional driver seeks to maintain rights to drive both buses and trucks professionally, they must complete 42 hours of periodic refresher training every five years. Periodic training must include a minimum of 7 hours training in a single day each year.

Drivers of the following vehicles are exempted, that is, the driver will not need to hold or carry a CPC:

- Vehicles not allowed to exceed 45 kilometres per hour;

- Vehicles used or controlled by the armed forces, civil defence, the fire service, the prison service and forces responsible for maintaining public order;

- Vehicles undergoing road tests for technical development, repair or maintenance, or new or rebuilt vehicles which have not been put into service;

- Vehicles used in states of emergency or for rescue missions;

- Vehicles used for driving lessons for anyone who wants to get a driving licence or a CPC;

- Vehicles used for carrying passengers or goods for personal use and not for business; and

- Vehicles carrying materials or equipment that the driver uses as part of their work, as long as driving the vehicle is not the driver's main activity.

Learner permit

A learner permit is issued to allow a person to learn to drive. Before you apply for your learner permit you **must** pass your driver theory test (see pages 17–18). In the interest of your safety and that of other road users, you **must** meet certain conditions attached to the learner permit, while you are driving. See Section 2 for more details.

You **must** have a current learner permit to learn to drive and to take your driving test. Your permit must be for the same category of vehicle as the one you will use in your test.

Driver theory test

The driver theory test applies to anyone applying for a first learner permit in any category. Note that it will be regarded as a first learner permit in the category if an earlier learner permit has expired by 5 years.

You must pass the driver theory test before applying for a learner permit.

The test is designed to check your knowledge of topics such as:

- Rules of the Road

- Risk perception

- Eco-driving

- Hazard awareness

- Good driving behaviour

The CPC theory test is designed to check your knowledge and understanding of all of the above and of 'safety loading' and 'vehicle security'.

The CPC driver theory tests for trucks and buses have been merged with the Driver CPC Step 1 exam and will each consist of 100 questions. There is also an option to sit both the truck and bus theory tests together. This combined theory test consists of 140 questions.

The test involves answering questions on a computer in a test centre. It is designed for people who have little or no experience of using computers as well as those who do. It is carried out by the Driver Theory Test Service. Those with special needs or disabilities can request a reader/recorder facility to help them complete the test.

The driver theory test study materials CD is available from all good book shops and from *www.theorytest.ie*. Further information on the fees for sitting the theory test and the locations of test centres is also available on the website.

You should check that you are using the most up-to-date study material.

All categories of licences are subject to review. To ensure compliance with EU and Irish road safety policy, you are advised to check the website *www.rsa.ie* regularly.

Applying for a first learner permit

When you apply for your learner permit, you **must** attend in person at any one of the National Driver Licence Services (NDLS) centres located around the country. You **must** allow your photograph to be taken for the purposes of your application when you attend at the NDLS centre. To apply for a learner permit, you **must** be able to demonstrate that you are normally resident in Ireland. If you are studying or working abroad, you may still be considered normally resident in Ireland provided you return here regularly.

The following table outlines what else you will need when applying for a learner permit. The categories of vehicles are described in the table on pages 11 to 13. Further information about the process of applying for a learner permit is available on the NDLS website, *www.ndls.ie*.

First learner permit

Category of first learner permit	What you need	
AM, A1, A2, A, B, W	• Application form • Appropriate fee • Theory Test Pass Certificate (must have been issued within 2 years of date of application)	• Evidence of identity • Evidence of residency entitlement, PPSN and address • Medical report, if applicable • Eyesight report
C1, C, D1 or D	• Application form • Appropriate fee • Theory Test Pass Certificate (note that this theory test will count as a Pass for the purposes of the Driver CPC Step 1)	• Evidence of PPSN and address (if changed since your last application) • Medical report (all applicants)* • Proof of full licence for category B vehicle
BE	• Application form • Appropriate fee • Theory Test, if applicable • Medical report, if applicable	• Evidence of PPSN and address (if changed since your last application) • Proof of full licence for category B vehicle
C1E, CE, D1E, DE	• Application form • Appropriate fee • Medical report (all applicants)* • Evidence of PPSN and address (if changed since your last application) • Evidence of Driver	Certificate of Professional Competence (if applicable) • Proof of full licence for the appropriate towing vehicle (for example category C if applying for a category CE licence)

* You will also need to have medical assessments from time to time when you have a full licence for these categories or when you renew.

Please note that what is needed for a first learner permit application can differ depending on your personal circumstances. Application requirements are also regularly updated. For these reasons, you are advised to visit the National Driver Licence Service website for details on what you need at the time of your application. See *www.ndls.ie*.

Eyesight and medical reports

- You can get eyesight and medical report forms from the National Driver Licence Service website, *www.ndls.ie*, or from the Road Safety Authority website, *www.rsa.ie*.

- A registered doctor or ophthalmic optician must fill in the eyesight report form.

- You must then sign it in front of them.

- A registered doctor must complete the medical report form.

- You must then sign it in front of them.

When you must supply a medical report

Not all applicants need to supply a medical report. However, you must supply one if any of the following statements applies to you.

- You are applying for a learner permit in any of the categories C1, C, D1, D, C1E, CE, D1E or DE.

- You will be 70 years of age or more on the first day the learner permit is being granted.

- You have any of the conditions listed in Appendix 1 at the back of this book.

- You are taking drugs or medications that are likely to affect your driving.

Note:

1. If you suffer from a serious medical condition, for example, an irregular or abnormally fast or slow heart beat (arrhythmia) that has ever caused you to lose consciousness, then make sure you visit a doctor before you apply for a learner permit or licence.

2. You are not allowed to hold a learner permit if you depend on or regularly abuse mind-altering substances.

Talk to your doctor if you have any doubts about your physical or mental fitness to drive.

You can get full details of the conditions attached to a learner permit on the National Driver Licence Service website, *www.ndls.ie*.

Learner permit expiration

No matter what type of vehicle you drive, you may get a third and subsequent learner permit only if you show that you have taken a driving test within the previous two years.

If you have not taken the test, you must give:

○ evidence that you have applied to sit your driving test for that category of vehicle, or

○ satisfy the NDLS that because of illness (as certified by a registered medical practitioner), you were not in a position to take a driving test.

'Six month rule'

If you are a first time holder of a learner permit for categories A, A2, A1, B, AM or W – that is, someone who never held a learner permit (or whose learner permit has expired by more than 5 years) in the category, you are not allowed to take a driving test for a six month period after the start date of your permit. This is to allow you to gain experience of driving. Research shows that the longer a learner is supervised while driving, the less likely they are to be involved in a collision.

The 'six month rule' does not apply to:

○ category BE vehicles;

○ the holder of a category A1 or A2 full licence who wishes to move progressively from the lower category of bike to the next higher category by having held the lower category for a minimum of 2 years;

○ the holder of a current full driving licence in the same category from another country for more than 6 months, provided the holder forwards a current original driving licence and a letter of entitlement to the RSA from the recognised licensing authority in that country.

If you have any questions about getting a learner permit, visit *www.ndls.ie* or contact the NDLS by email at *info@ndls.ie* or through their Customer Services at 076 1087 880.

Full driving licence

You need a full driving licence for the category of vehicle that you intend to drive. You can drive only the category or categories of vehicle for which the licence is issued.

Examples of full driving licence

Old style   New style

Applying for your full licence

You **must** apply for your driving licence in person at any one of the National Driver Licence Service (NDLS) centres located around the country. When attending your appointment at the NDLS centre, you **must** bring with you:

- a completed application form;

- the relevant fee;

- your current or most recent learner permit; and

- evidence of your PPSN and address (if changed) dated within last 6 months.

You **must** allow your photograph to be taken for the purposes of your application.

With the application for your first licence, you **must** include your certificate of competency to drive (outlined in Section 3). You may also need to supply other documents, such as a medical report, depending on your circumstances. A licence will not be granted to you if you have a driving licence which has been restricted, suspended or withdrawn in another EU Member State or a country recognised for driving licence exchange.

To apply for a driving licence, you **must** be able to demonstrate that you are normally resident in Ireland. If you are studying or working abroad, you may still be considered normally resident in Ireland provided you return here regularly.

You can get more information about applying for your full licence on the National Driver Licence Service (NDLS) website, *www.ndls.ie*.

Novice drivers

Remember to check the rules on displaying 'N' plates for novice drivers to see if they apply to you. If you are a first time holder of a full driving licence, you will be considered a 'novice driver' for 2 years from the date you received your first full licence.

As a novice driver, you **must** display N-plates on your vehicle for 2 years. N-plates must be displayed on any vehicle you get a licence to drive during that 2-year period.

This novice period applies only once. For example, if you hold a driving licence for a category of vehicle and after 2 years you become entitled to drive another category of vehicle, you do not become a 'novice driver' in respect of the new category.

Novice drivers do not have to have an accompanying driver (but remember that this is still the case for learner drivers). However, a novice driver **should not** act as an accompanying driver for someone who holds a learner permit. If a learner driver is found driving without an appropriately qualified driver (that is, a person who has held a full driving licence in the same category for a continuous period of 2 years), the learner driver has committed an offence and is liable for a fixed-charge fine or penalty points, or both.

You can get further information about the N-plate requirements on the Road Safety Authority's website, *www.rsa.ie*.

Renewing your licence

A driving licence is normally valid for 10 years for cars and motorcycles or 5 years for trucks and buses; you should renew your licence before this period passes. To renew your licence, you **must** apply in person to one of the NDLS centres . You will need to bring:

- a completed application form and fee,
- your current or most recent full licence, and
- evidence of your PPSN and address (if changed) dated within last 6 months.

If you are renewing a category C1, C1E (previously EC1), C, CE (previously EC), D1, D1E (previously ED1), D or DE (previously ED) licence, you **must** include a medical report.

You **should** apply to renew your licence not later than three months before it expires.

If you hold a foreign valid licence from an EU/EEA country or other 'recognised state', it may be possible to exchange your licence for a full Irish driving licence.

You can get full details about renewing or exchanging your driving licence on the National Driver Licence Service website, *www.ndls.ie.*

Carrying a driving licence

Remember, you **must** carry your driving licence, or learner permit as appropriate (all categories), with you at all times when you are driving.

Driving legally

Before taking any vehicle on to the road you **must** be able to answer 'yes' to the following questions:

- Are you carrying your driving licence or learner permit?
- Is the motor vehicle taxed?
- Is the tax disc on the windscreen?
- Is the insurance cover up to date and valid to cover you?
- Is the insurance disc on the windscreen?
- Is there an N-plate sign at the front and rear of your vehicle? (if you are a novice driver)

○ Is the vehicle roadworthy and does it have an up-to-date National Car Test (NCT) Certificate on the windscreen? (if you are learning to drive a category B vehicle that is over four years old but not a taxi)

○ Does the vehicle have a Certificate of Roadworthiness? (if you are using a coach, bus, ambulance, goods vehicle or goods trailer and it is over a year old)

○ Are you carrying your CPC qualification card (as required)? (if you are a professional driver)

IMPORTANT MESSAGE TO OVERSEAS DRIVERS

You must drive on the left-hand side of the road in Ireland.

Tax

All motor vehicles **must** be taxed before the vehicle is taken on the road.

Insurance

All drivers **must** have insurance covering them to drive a vehicle in a public place. By law you must inform the insurance company of relevant information, such as important changes in your medical fitness to drive, before you drive a vehicle. If you are in any doubt you **should** discuss the matter with the insurance company. It is a serious offence to drive a vehicle that is not insured.

You need to display an up-to-date insurance disc. It is an offence not to have the disc on display.

Vehicles that do not need to display an insurance disc

- Motorcycles (with or without a side car)
- Tractors
- Vehicles showing a trade licence
- Vehicles owned or used by an exempted person as defined by the Road Traffic Acts, for example members of emergency services

All trailers **must** be covered by third party motor insurance. This applies whether the trailer is being towed or parked in a public place.

Even though the trailer does not have to display an insurance disc, you must have valid insurance cover.

National car test

Vehicle testing makes sure your vehicle is safe to use on the road. This is especially important for older vehicles.

- Passenger cars over 4 years old **must** have a valid NCT Certificate and show the NCT disc on the windscreen;
- Passenger cars under ten years old **must** be tested every 2 years;
- Passenger cars over ten years old **must** be tested every year;
- You may also avail of 'voluntary early testing' and get your car tested earlier than 90 days before its NCT due date.

Further information on the NCT is available on the National Car Testing Service website, *www.ncts.ie*.

Commercial vehicle roadworthiness test

Commercial vehicles must pass a Commercial Vehicle Roadworthiness (CVR) test every year. The purpose of this test is to assess the roadworthiness of a commercial vehicle on the day of the test.

Goods vehicles, goods trailers with a design gross vehicle weight of more than 3,500kg, ambulances, buses (including minibuses) and coaches must have a valid Certificate of Roadworthiness.

As an owner of a commercial vehicle, you must:

- inspect, maintain and repair your vehicle regularly and perform daily walk around checks of your vehicle in order to maintain a commercial vehicle in a safe and roadworthy condition over its lifetime;

- keep records of reported defects, maintenance and repair;

- nominate a 'Suitably Qualified Person' (SQP) to be responsible for carrying out inspection and maintenance of your vehicles and any repairs needed to rectify defects on your vehicles or trailers.

The SQP can be a mechanic or equivalent person with the relevant experience or qualifications to enable them to assess the roadworthiness of a vehicle and carry out any necessary repairs.

All Heavy Commercial Vehicle (HCV) owners/operators are required to complete and submit an online self-declaration every year to the RSA providing details such as:

- Number of vehicles in your fleet and their details;

- Any safety inspections and maintenance controls;

- Name of the relevant person who is responsible for vehicle maintenance.

You can get more information about the Certificate of Roadworthiness and testing requirements on the Commercial Vehicle Roadworthiness test website, *www.cvrt.ie*.

Certificate of Professional Competence

Professional bus and truck drivers must also carry their Driver CPC qualification card.

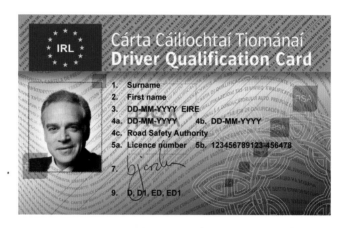

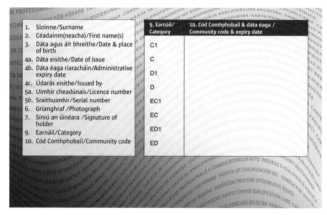

1. Sloinne/Surname	9. Earnáil/	10. Cód Comhphobail & dáta éaga /
2. Céadainm(neacha)/First name(s)	Category	Community code & expiry date
3. Dáta agus áit bhreithe/Date & place of birth	C1	
4a. Dáta eisithe/Date of issue	C	
4b. Dáta éaga riaracháin/Administrative expiry date	D1	
4c. Údarás eisithe/Issued by	D	
5a. Uimhir cheadúnais/Licence number		
5b. Sraithuimhir/Serial number	EC1	
6. Grianghraf /Photograph	EC	
7. Síniú an úinéara /Signature of holder	ED1	
9. Earnáil/Category		
10. Cód Comhphobail/Community code	ED	

Section 2:
The learner driver

///

The Road Safety Authority has produced a suite of manuals to help learners as they learn to drive a car, a truck or a bus, or ride a motorcycle.

Conditions for learner permit holders

When you are a learner driver you must, in addition to answering yes to the questions on page 23, comply with the following conditions:

1) Accompanied when driving

- A holder of a learner permit for categories B, BE, C, C1, C1E, CE, D, D1, D1E and DE must be accompanied and supervised at all times by a qualified driver. A qualified driver is a person who has held a full driving licence in the same category for a continuous period of 2 years. It is an offence for a learner driver to drive unaccompanied by a qualified driver. This offence attracts a penalty of a fixed charge and up to 4 penalty points.

- A holder of a learner permit for category AM, A1, A2 and A does not need to be accompanied by a qualified driver. However, you cannot drive a vehicle in this category unsupervised by your Initial Basic Training (IBT) instructor until you have completed the IBT for your relevant category and type of motorcycle.

2) 'L' Plates

- Learner permit holders for all categories (except W) must display 'L' plates while they are driving. It is an offence for a learner driver to drive without displaying 'L' plates. This offence attracts a penalty of a fixed charge fine and up to 4 penalty points.

- Learner permit holders for categories A, A1, A2 and AM must display 'L' plates on a yellow fluorescent tabard that are clearly visible on the front and back of the driver's body.

3) Essential Driver Training and Initial Basic Training

It is illegal to give driving instruction for payment or reward to learner drivers if you are not registered with the Road Safety Authority. A list of all Approved Driving Instructors (ADI) is available on *www.rsa.ie*.

4) Car Driver Training

All holders of their first learner permit issued from 4 April 2011 must undertake Essential Driver Training (EDT) with an Approved Driving Instructor (ADI). [See *www.rsa.ie* for an up to date list of ADIs.]

EDT is a training course that teaches fundamental driving skills to learner car drivers. The course is made up of 12 individual one hour lessons.

At your first EDT lesson, your ADI will check your learner permit, and if you are using your own car, will check to make sure your insurance, motor tax, NCT and roadworthiness of the vehicle are all in order. In addition, your ADI will give you your official EDT logbook which you are responsible for and should take along to each lesson. The logbook must be completed including an official stamp and instructor's signature.

A Sponsor is a qualified driver who must supervise any driving practice outside of formal lessons and track practice sessions in your logbook.

Be sure to confirm with your ADI what type of lesson you are booking for your next lesson. Not all lessons are EDT.

5) Motorcycles and Initial Basic Training

Since 6 December 2010 all new first time learner permit holders for motorcycles must undertake Initial Basic Training (IBT) with an approved IBT instructor, before they can ride a motorcycle unsupervised.

IBT is a training course that teaches basic riding skills to learner motorcyclists. IBT is a 16-hour course broken into 4 modules focusing on theory and practical skills, to be taken in sequence.

When you have completed each IBT Module of your IBT course, your instructor will record the details of your training in your logbook. Once all modules have been completed, your ADI will issue you with a Certificate of Satisfactory Completion.

Section 3:
The driving test

///

How to apply for your driving test

Once you have learnt to drive safely and completed mandatory training (EDT for category B or IBT for Category AM, A1, A2 or A) the next step is to apply for your driving test.

Note: bus drivers and truck drivers should refer to page 15 for the CPC Driving Test.

You can apply and pay for your driving test online at www.rsa.ie. You will need a credit or debit card and a valid email address to complete the application online.

Alternatively, you can download a driving test form from *www.rsa.ie* or get one from your local Garda station. Send the completed form, with a cheque, postal order or money order made payable to the Road Safety Authority to:

Driver Testing Section
Road Safety Authority, Moy Valley Business Park, Primrose Hill, Dublin Road, Ballina, Co. Mayo.

Remember

To take a Driving Test you **must**:

- Hold a learner permit for the vehicle in which you wish to be tested;

- Have use of a suitable vehicle;

- Comply with the 6-month rule – that is, you must have held a valid learner permit for at least 6 months on the day of the test (this applies to cars, motorcycles and work vehicles);

- There are certain exceptions to the 6-month rule. For example, learner permit holders in category BE (car/van and trailer) do not need to wait 6 months before undergoing a practical driving test in that category. See further exceptions to the 6 month rule at page 32.

Also, if your first Category B learner permit was issued on or after 4 April 2011 you must:

- have completed an Essential Driver Training (EDT) course;

- have completed an Initial Basic Training (IBT) course if your first Category A type learner permit was issued on or after 6 December 2010.

What you need to do on the day of the test

The following information is a summary of requirements. The notification of your test appointment contains all the relevant information and requirements which must be met on the day.

- Use the correct vehicle for your test.

  - Under current regulations specific guidelines set out the minimum requirements for a vehicle to be acceptable for use by you during a driving test (see appendix 5). You will be advised of the vehicle requirements on your test appointment notice. However, if you have any concerns, please refer to *www.rsa.ie* where full details are available.

- Make sure your vehicle displays:

  - a current valid motor tax disc;

  - a valid NCT disc or CVRT disc, as applicable to your vehicle (see page 26);

  - proper 'L' plates at the front and back, (other than Category A, A1, A2 and AM where you wear the plates on your person); and

  - a current valid insurance disc (except if you are being tested in a category A, A1, A2, AM and W vehicle).

- Make sure your vehicle is roadworthy.

- Be in the test centre at least 10 minutes before your test appointment time.

- Give the driver tester your current Irish learner permit. The tester will check the permit to confirm that it relates to you, is current and is for the correct category of vehicle.

- Read the 'Checklist for your driving test' on *www.rsa.ie*.

Your test will be cancelled and you will lose your fee if:

- you are late;

- your vehicle does not show the correct discs or L plates;

- your vehicle is not roadworthy; or

- you do not have the correct vehicle for your test (see Appendix 5).

You can get more information from *www.rsa.ie*.

The driving test

The driving test will determine if you have the skills necessary to get your full driving licence. The test includes questions on the Rules of the Road and how your vehicle works. It assesses your driving skills while you drive in different road and traffic conditions.

The Driver Tester will evaluate your driving knowledge and skills and will use an electronic device to make notes during your test. Following your driving test, you will receive an email about your result which you should discuss with your Approved Driving Instructor. They will be able to help you to interpret the report and they will be able to give you advice on how to keep improving your driving.

The driving test will evaluate your driving skills under various headings, including:

- positioning the vehicle correctly and in good time;

- taking proper observation;

- reacting promptly and properly to hazards;

- using mirrors properly, in good time and before signalling;

- allowing sufficient clearance to pedestrians, cyclists, other traffic, and so on;

- giving correct signals in good time;

- maintaining reasonable progress and avoiding undue hesitancy when moving off, at roundabouts, changing lanes, and so on;

- making proper use of vehicle controls;

- adjusting speed appropriately;

- complying with traffic controls, for example, traffic lights, traffic signs, road marking, and so on;

- yielding right of way as required;

- reversing;

- turnabout; and

- parking.

Before taking the test, you **should** have achieved a level of knowledge and skill that will satisfy the tester that you are entitled to a full licence.

The requirements for the test process will change on an ongoing basis, so to make yourself aware of any changes, visit *www.rsa.ie*.

The following table highlights some recent changes. Some requirements apply to more than one type of vehicle.

If you are being tested for:	Category	You must know how to:
A car	B	• Demonstrate technical checks. • Work the secondary controls. • Adjust the seat, seat-belt, head restraint, mirrors. • Ensure the doors are closed.
A motorcycle	AM, A1, A2, A	• Demonstrate technical checks. • Remove and replace the machine from its stand. • Adjust your protective outfit (personal safety equipment). • Move the motorcycle without the aid of the engine. • Drive in such a way as to ensure safety and reduce fuel consumption and emissions while performing certain manoeuvres.
A trailer	BE	• Demonstrate technical checks. • Connect and remove the trailer to or from your vehicle. • Reverse up to a loading bay. • Park safely for loading/unloading.
A heavy vehicle	C, C1, CE, CE1	• Demonstrate technical checks. • Work the secondary controls. • Use any retarder or exhaust brake fitted to the vehicle. • Reverse up to a loading bay. • Park safely for loading/unloading at a loading ramp, platform or similar area.
A bus	D, D1, DE, DE1	• Demonstrate technical checks. • Work the secondary controls. • Use any retarder or exhaust brake fitted to the vehicle. • Open and close by hand any powered doors fitted to the vehicle. • Demonstrate instrument panel and recording equipment check.

Secondary controls and technical checks

At your test, you will have to:

- work the secondary controls, such as windscreen wipers and washers, de-misters, rear window heater, lights and air-conditioning, fans, rear foglights, air vents and temperature control.

- demonstrate technical checks such as air pressure and the condition of tyres, oil, fuel, windscreen washer fluid level, coolant, brakes (including handbrake), steering, lights, indicators, reflectors and horn.

The Driving Test Report Form explains the technical checks and the secondary controls in detail. Make yourself familiar with the content of the Driving Test Report Form.

Motorcyclists are further tested on: control of speed, control when braking and avoiding obstacles.

How long does the test last?

The test for categories A, A1, A2, AM, B, BE and W vehicles lasts about 40 minutes and assesses your driving skills over a distance of about eight to ten kilometres.

The test for vehicles in other categories lasts about 70 minutes and assesses your driving skills over about 20 kilometres.

What happens when your test is finished?

If you pass, the tester will give you a Certificate of Competency to drive. You should change it for your full driving licence as soon as possible and you must change it within two years of your cert date.

If you are a novice driver (that is, you are a first-time holder of a full driving licence), you must display N-plates on your vehicle for a period of 2 years. N-plates must be displayed on any vehicle you get a licence to drive during that 2-year period. This novice period applies only once. For example, if you hold a driving licence for a category of vehicle and after two years you get a licence to drive another category of vehicle, you do not become a 'novice driver' in respect of the new category. You can get further information about the N-plate requirements on the Road Safety Authority website, *www.rsa.ie.*

Your Certificate of Competency will list any restrictions to be applied to your licence. Any restrictions will be shown on your driving licence by using a particular code. Further information on potential restrictions on a driving licence is available on the RSA website, *www.rsa.ie.*

If you are not successful in your driving test, you will receive a detailed report on the faults that occurred during the test. When you are preparing for your next test, pay particular attention to these faults while continuing to work on other areas of your driving.

What to do if you are not happy with your test result

If you were not successful and believe that your driving test was not conducted properly or fairly, you may appeal the tester's decision to the District Court. The District Court may either refuse the appeal or, if it finds that the test was not properly conducted, it can direct the Road Safety Authority to give you another test free of charge.

For more information on the driving test, please read the leaflet *Preparing for your Driving Test*. This is available at *www.rsa.ie*.

Since January 2013, it may be possible, in certain circumstances, to progress to a higher category of driving licence for motorcycles without having to undergo an additional driving test. This is known as 'progressive access'.

At the age of 24 years, a rider may also proceed directly to a large unrestricted motorcycle. This is known as 'direct access'.

Section 4:
Vehicle safety

///

There are minimum standards set by law for the condition of your vehicle. You **must** know these standards and make sure your vehicle complies with the law. This section sets out the basic information you need to know. For further information on the testing of your vehicle please see *www.rsa.ie*.

As a driver, you **must** make sure that your vehicle is in good working order. You **must** ensure that the steering, brakes, front and rear lamps, indicators, reflectors, rear view mirrors, safety belts, speedometer, tyres, windscreen wipers, horn and silencer are checked regularly.

As an owner of a commercial vehicle, you **must** put in place a system for the regular inspection and on-going maintenance of your vehicle and ensure it has a valid Certificate of Roadworthiness. This involves implementing the following measures:

- deciding how often a vehicle is to be inspected, taking into account the age, mileage and condition of the vehicle;

- ensuring a daily walk-around check of the vehicle is performed before it is driven in a public place, which involves the inspection of both the inside and outside of the vehicle as well as examination of various items such as the mirrors, seatbelts, tyres, exhaust, and so on;

- keeping records of all inspections, maintenance and repairs of the vehicle.

For further details on the Commercial Vehicle Roadworthiness Test (CVRT), see *www.cvrt.ie*.

The RSA advise motorists that it would be useful to have the following items available for use in your vehicle:

- a first aid kit.

- at least 1 high-viz vest or jacket (fluorescent and reflective).

- at least 1 red warning triangle (this is required for HGVs and buses).

- a torch.

The above are examples of items that might be useful in an emergency. You might choose to carry other items that you feel might be helpful.

REMEMBER

It is an offence to drive an unsafe vehicle on a public road.

Motor vehicles **must** be tested for their roadworthiness. This section sets out the minimum standards required for your vehicle. You **should** check the following on a regular basis:

Tyres

Tread depth: Do not allow your tyres to wear down too much. Most vehicles on the road **must** have a minimum tread depth of 1.6mm over the main treads. For motorcycles and vintage vehicles the minimum tread depth is 1mm. However, make sure you replace your tyres before they become this worn.

Pressure: Regularly check the pressure of every tyre, including the spare tyre, and pay attention to the recommended pressure levels. See the manufacturer's specifications for correct inflation pressure.

Checking for damage: Regularly examine your tyres for cuts, cracks and bulges, which could cause unexpected 'blow-outs.'

Replacing tyres: For your safety only fit new and e-marked tyres bought from a reputable dealer. Do not mix radial and cross ply tyres on any one axle. Tyres must be the same on any axle.

Temporary use (space saver) spare tyres: Only use these tyres to complete a journey or make a journey to a tyre dealer. Do not travel at a speed in excess of the recommended speed stamped on the tyre.

REMEMBER

Use of secondhand tyres can be risky and should be avoided because there is no history of how they have been used or abused.

Lights and reflectors

Motor vehicles (except motorcycles or electric vehicles with a maximum speed of 38km/h) **must** have the following lights and reflectors:

At the front:

- Two headlights (white or yellow)
- Two white sidelights
- Direction indicator lights (amber only)

At the back:

- Two red lights (commonly known as tail lights)
- Two red brake lights
- Two red reflectors
- Number plate lighting
- Direction indicator lights (amber only)

Remember:

- You **must** only use fog lights in dense fog or falling snow. Turn them off in clear weather or you will risk causing glare and may dazzle other drivers.

- You may fit high mounted rear brake lights if you wish, but fitting other optional lighting is controlled by law.

Sections 16, 17 and 20 deal with the required lighting for motorcycles, bicycles and horse-drawn vehicles.

Before you change or alter the physical appearance of your vehicle, for example by fitting spot lights, bull bars or ornaments, take care not to increase the risk to road users, in particular the more vulnerable ones, for example cyclists and pedestrians.

The use of flashing lights, with the exception of direction indicators, is solely reserved for Gardaí, ambulance and other designated service vehicles. You **must not** fit blue or red flashing lights to your vehicle. See *www.dttas.ie* for details.

A vehicle **must** have white or yellow lights showing to the front and red lights showing to the rear, together with amber direction indicators and white or yellow reverse lamps.

You **should not** make any technical modifications to your vehicle without professional advice as these may have legal and safety implications.

You **should** also inform your insurance company, as some modifications can invalidate your insurance policy.

It is recommended that dipped headlights only be used when driving or when stopped in traffic. Avoid having them switched on when stopped at the side of the road. You **should not** use headlights when parked. If you need lights when parked or stopped, it is recommended that you use 'side' lights or 'parking' lights.

REMEMBER

Please note that specific reflective markings must **be displayed on HGVs and their trailers. Please see *www.rsa.ie* for further information.**

Windscreens

Type of windscreen: Laminated glass must be used for the windscreens of motor vehicles registered since January 1986. It must also be used when replacing damaged windscreens of older vehicles.

Windscreen wipers: Keep your windscreen wipers and wiper blades in good working condition and keep your windscreen washer liquid topped up.

Clear vision: Keep your windscreen and windows clean and free of clutter to make sure you can see the road and other road users clearly.

Mirrors

Your vehicle must have mirrors fitted so that you always know what is behind (rear-view) and to each side (door or wing mirrors).

On large vehicles the fitment of a front mirror, known as a Cyclops mirror, has the potential to reduce fatalities and serious injuries from collisions between HGVs and cyclists or pedestrians.

All HGVs must have Cyclops, close proximity and wide-angle mirrors to eliminate 'blind spots' and protect pedestrians and cyclists to the front and sides of the vehicles. This requirement also applies to buses where they have been fitted by the original manufacturer as part of the vehicles type approval process.

Note:

HGVs registered after 2007 are obliged to have these safety-enhancing mirrors.

From 1 October 2012, the HGV annual roadworthiness test includes a check for conformance with the new regulations.

Further details are available at *www.rsa.ie*.

Additional information is also available from *vehiclestandards@rsa.ie* or alternately at 096-25014.

When to use mirrors: You must use your vehicle's mirrors before signalling, when moving off, changing lanes, overtaking, slowing down, stopping, turning, or opening doors.

In addition, you **should** check your mirrors regularly whilst driving to observe what is going on behind your vehicle.

Clear vision: As with lights and reflectors, you must keep your mirrors clean, in good condition and correctly positioned to make sure they are effective.

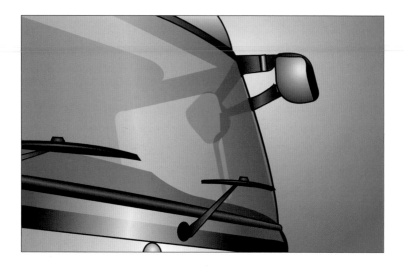

Safety belts

Where fitted, you **must** wear a safety belt. The only exceptions are for:

- people who wear a disabled person's belt,
- people whose doctors have certified that, on medical grounds, they should not wear a safety belt,
- driving instructors or driver testers during a lesson or a test, and
- Gardaí or members of the Defence Forces in the course of their duty.

Private buses and heavy goods vehicles registered since 20 October 2007 **must** have seat belts fitted.

Bus owners are required to present documentation at their bus roadworthiness test certifying that the seat belts, where fitted to their vehicle, meet a minimum standard.

Since October 2011, all buses involved in the organised transport of children are required to be fitted with certified seat belt installations. This requirement does not apply to the transport of children on bus services offered to the general public (scheduled urban or inter-urban bus services).

Child restraint systems

Safety belts are designed mainly for adults and older children. Child safety protection laws make it compulsory for all children to use the correct child seat, booster seat or booster cushion. Smaller children – under 150 centimetres tall and less than 36 kilograms in weight – must be restrained in an appropriate child restraint system when travelling in a passenger car or goods vehicle. Examples of appropriate restraint systems are baby car seats and booster seats.

You must comply with the following:

- Where safety belts have been fitted, they must be worn.

- Children under 3 years of age must not travel in a car or goods vehicle (other than a taxi) unless restrained in the correct child seat.

- Children aged 3 years or over who are under 150cms in height and weigh less than 36 kilograms (generally children up to 11 or 12 years old) must use the correct child seat or booster cushion when travelling in cars or goods vehicles.

- Children over 3 years of age must travel in a rear seat in vehicles not fitted with safety belts.

- A rearward-facing child car seat must not be used in the front passenger seat of cars with active airbags.

- A child car seat must be in accordance with EU or United Nations – Economic Commission for Europe (UN-ECE) standards.

- Make sure passengers aged under 17 use the correct seat, booster seat, booster cushion or seatbelt. All drivers are legally responsible for this.

It is an offence to fail to comply with the above outlined child restraint system requirements. Specifically, it is an offence for a driver to:

- allow a person under 17 years of age to occupy a seat without wearing a seatbelt,

- allow a child under 3 years of age to travel in a vehicle without being restrained by an appropriate child restraint,

- allow a child over 3 years of age to travel in a vehicle without being restrained by an appropriate child restraint,

- allow a child to be restrained by a rearward-facing child restraint fitted to a seat which is protected by an active frontal air-bag.

These offences attract a fixed charge and/or up to 5 penalty points.

Ensuring a child is properly restrained in a child car seat can reduce injuries by a factor of 90-95% for rear-facing seats and 60% for forward-facing seats*.

*Source: AA Motoring Trust

Never put a rearward facing seat in the front seat, if there is a passenger airbag.

Rearward-facing baby seat
Weight: for babies up to 13kgs (29lbs)
Approximate age range: birth to 12-15 months

Forward-facing child seat
Weight: 9-18kgs (20-40lbs)
Approximate age range: 9mths to 4 years

Booster seat
Weight: 15-23kgs (33-55lbs)
Approximate age range: 4-6 years

Fixing cushion
Weight: 22-36kgs (48-79lbs)
Approximate age range: 6-12 years

What to remember when using child restraints

○ Use the correct restraint for each child.

○ Use the child seat for every journey, no matter how short.

○ For young children, choose a seat that:

  • bears an E mark (meaning that it meets United Nations Standard ECE Regulation 44 03),

  • suits the child's weight and height, and

  • is suitable for the type of car.

○ The best advice is not to buy or use a second hand car seat.

○ Fit the child seat correctly, according to the manufacturer's instructions. It is safer to fit the seat in the back seat of your car.

It is recommended that you buy a child car seat only from a retailer who will check that it fits. Make sure it fits your child and your car. For further information go to *www.rsa.ie*.

Restraints for passengers under 17

By law, the driver of a passenger car or goods vehicle must ensure passengers under 17 years of age wear a safety belt or an appropriate child restraint. You may receive up to 5 penalty points if your passengers in this age group are not belted or restrained.

If you would like more information, you can get a booklet and DVD called *Child Safety in Cars* from the Road Safety Authority. Check the RSA website for more details, *www.rsa.ie*.

Roof racks and roof boxes

If you use a roof rack or roof box, you must:

○ securely fit it to your vehicle,

○ make sure that the load does not block your view of the road in any direction,

○ never overload it,

○ never place the load in a way that might cause it to fall off, and

○ never load the rack or box in a way that would destabilise your vehicle.

To be safe, you **are strongly advised** to check that the roof rack or box is correctly mounted and the load is completely secured before you set off. These checks also apply if you are using a rear or roof-mounted bicycle rack.

Vehicle registration plates

The law sets down what vehicle registration plates must look like. The two diagrams below show the only formats that are allowed for vehicles registered in Ireland on or after 1 January 1991.

Diagram 1:   *Diagram 2:*

Vehicle registration plates must be kept clean and legible. All numbers and letters must be in plain black text on a plain white reflective background. There **should** be no italics or shadows. You must not interfere with a registration plate.

If you would like more information on vehicle plates, you can get a leaflet from the following page on Revenue's website: *http://www.revenue.ie/en/tax/vrt/ leaflets/format-vehicle-registration-plates.html*

Other safety responsibilities

As a driver, you have a number of other responsibilities to your passengers.

Children in motor vehicles

You must not leave infants or young children on their own in a motor vehicle, even if you are only away for a short time. The children may face a number of hazards, such as:

- a fire breaking out,
- difficulty in breathing on a warm day (if all windows are closed), and
- being trapped in electric windows, which could result in serious injury or death.

Animals in motor vehicles

You **should** never leave animals alone in vehicles. It is cruel and unsafe and can result in injury to the animal and/or damage to your vehicle.

Using a mobile phone

You must not drive a vehicle or ride a motorbike while using a hand-held mobile phone. It is an offence, for which you may receive a fixed charge and/or up to 5 penalty points.

You must not send a text message or email or read a text message or email from a mobile phone while driving a vehicle or riding a motorbike. It is an offence for which a person will face a compulsory court appearance and a fine to be determined by the judge. There is also the possibility of a prison term of up to 3 months to be imposed in cases of multiple offences in a 12-month period. There is no option to take the lesser penalty of penalty points for this offence.

You may only use your mobile phone when you are driving if you are phoning 999 or 112, or you are responding to another type of genuine emergency.

Cyclists **should** never use a mobile phone when cycling and pedestrians **should** be careful when using one.

Personal entertainment systems

As a road user, you **should** avoid using personal entertainment systems through earphones. These systems – for example, personal radios and MP3 players – can distract you, and may prove dangerous when driving or crossing the road. Cyclists in particular **should** avoid these systems, as cyclists rely on their hearing while on the road.

If you do use a personal or in-car system, play it at a volume that does not distract or prevent you from hearing emergency sirens or car horns.

Section 5:
Good driving practice

//

This section describes how to do the most common driving manoeuvres safely and with consideration for other road users. It focuses on:

- ○ moving off,
- ○ your position on the road,
- ○ changing traffic lanes,
- ○ overtaking,
- ○ reversing,
- ○ u-turns,
- ○ slowing down or stopping,
- ○ towing,
- ○ day time running lights,
- ○ driving at night, and
- ○ using a horn.

Moving off

- ○ Before moving off, carry out the following safety checks:
  - • check that all doors, the bonnet and the boot are closed;
  - • make sure your seat and head restraint are properly adjusted;
  - • make sure your rear view mirrors are clean and properly adjusted; and
  - • check that all safety belts (yours and those of your front-seat and back-seat passengers) are fastened.
- ○ When moving off from the kerb, you **must** signal and give way to other traffic as well as any pedestrians.

- When the way is clear, move out and adjust your speed to that of the normal safe and legal flow of traffic.

- Always look in your mirror but remember that there are blind spots, so always check over your shoulders as well. Traffic and pedestrians may be coming up beside your vehicle. When moving off from a stationary position check your blind spots by looking around you.

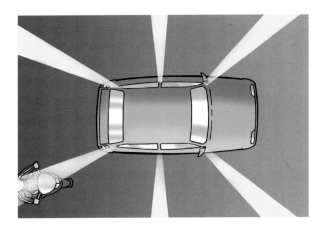

- When you are ready to move off, check your mirrors and signal your intention to move out into traffic.

Your position on the road

Make sure you drive your vehicle far enough to the left to allow traffic to safely pass or overtake on the right, but not so far to the left that you are driving on a cycle lane or blocking or endangering cyclists or pedestrians.

What to do if you need to change your road position

- If you are overtaking, turning right or passing pedestrians, cyclists, horse riders, other road users or parked vehicles, make sure it is safe to do so.

- Always check in your mirror for any vehicles coming up on your right or overtaking from behind, and don't forget to check your blind spots.

- Give a clear signal to warn traffic in good time of your intentions and proceed.

Taking care with buses and pedestrians

You **should** allow signalling buses back into the stream of traffic after they let passengers on and off. Be especially careful of pedestrians getting on and off buses and of children near schools. When driving near schools, always be prepared to stop. It is advisable to drive your vehicle in a defensive manner, be prepared to stop, sound the horn and brake. Always expect the unexpected.

Taking care with cyclists

If you are at a junction where there is an advanced stop line for cyclists, you **should** allow cyclists to move off ahead of you.

When turning left, all drivers, especially drivers of heavy goods vehicles, must watch out for cyclists and motorcyclists going ahead or turning.

On left turns, watch out for cyclists and mopeds close to the kerb in front of you or coming up on your left. Do not overtake a cyclist as you approach a junction if you are turning left, as the cyclist might be continuing straight ahead.

It is recommended that you give extra space (at least 1.5 metres) when overtaking a cyclist, as they may need to avoid uneven road surfaces and obstacles. This is particularly important on wet or windy days.

Changing traffic lanes

Don't move from one traffic lane to another without good reason.

You must give way to traffic already in the lane into which you are moving.

REMEMBER

Signalling does not give you the right of way.

How to change lanes safely

- If you have good reason to change lanes, use your mirrors and check in plenty of time to ensure that the way is clear. To check your blind spot when travelling at speed, take a quick sideways glance to check the position of a vehicle that may have disappeared from your view in the mirror.

- Signal your intention and change lane when it is clear and safe to do so.

- When in a lane or approaching a junction, obey any road signs or markings (usually arrows) indicating the direction that traffic in those lanes must take.

Overtaking

Only overtake if it is safe for you and other road users. Be particularly careful of features that may hinder your view of the road ahead, such as hills, dips, bends, bridges, pedestrian crossings or roads narrowing. Pay attention to the rules on road signs or markings (continuous, broken, single, double white lines) covered in Section 6.

How to overtake safely

Make sure the road ahead is clear so you have enough distance to overtake and get back to your own side of the road without forcing any other road user to move to avoid you.

- Never directly follow another overtaking vehicle.

- Give way to faster traffic already overtaking from behind.

- Before overtaking check that the way is clear, check in your mirror and check your blind spots to ensure another vehicle is not approaching from behind. Give your signal in good time, move out when it is safe to do so, accelerate and overtake with the minimum of delay.

- When you are well past, check the mirror, signal and gradually move in again making sure not to cut across the vehicle you have passed.

- Take extra care when overtaking a vehicle displaying a 'LONG VEHICLE' sign. This means that the vehicle is at least 13 metres long and you will need extra road length to pass it and safely return to the left-hand side of the road.

- You must not break the speed limit, even when overtaking.

> ### REMEMBER
>
> **You must normally overtake on the right. However, you are allowed to overtake on the left in the situations listed below.**

You may overtake on the left when

- You want to go straight ahead when the driver in front of you has moved out and signalled that they intend to turn right.
- You have signalled that you intend to turn left.
- Traffic in both lanes is moving slowly but traffic in the left-hand lane is moving more quickly than the right-hand lane – for example, in slow moving stop/start traffic conditions.

You must not overtake when

- You are at or near a pelican crossing, zebra crossing or at pedestrian signals.
- A traffic sign or road marking prohibits it.
- You are approaching a junction.
- You are on the approach to a corner, bend, dip in the road, hump-back bridge, brow of a hill or on a narrow road.

- You are in the left-hand lane of a dual carriageway or motorway when traffic is moving at normal speed.

- It would at any time cause danger or inconvenience to another road user.

What to do when somebody overtakes you

- Continue at the same pace, unless it becomes unsafe to do so.

- Keep as near to the left as is safe.

- Do not accelerate.

- Be alert in case the overtaking vehicle suddenly pulls back in front of you.

Reversing

How to reverse safely

- Check for nearby pedestrians and traffic by looking carefully all around, in front of and behind you, over both your shoulders and in your mirrors.

- Take special care where small children may be gathered, such as schools, playgrounds, residential roads, car parks or your own driveway.

- If your view is restricted, ask for help when reversing.

- Give way to other traffic or pedestrians.

- When reversing from a major road onto a minor road, wait until it is safe, reverse slowly far enough into the side road to allow you to take up the correct position on the left-hand side when rejoining the major road.

- Take extra care when reversing if it is dark.

- If you are in doubt, get out of your vehicle and check the area.

- You must not reverse from a minor road onto a major road as it is unsafe to do so.

U-turns

You must not make a U-turn unless traffic conditions make it completely safe to do so.

○ Check there are no signs or road markings prohibiting a U-turn, for example a continuous centre white line.

○ Check that the road is not one way.

○ Look for a safe place, where you can see clearly in all directions.

○ Give way to all other road users.

○ Check carefully for cyclists and motorcyclists.

○ Do not delay or prevent pedestrians from crossing safely.

○ Make sure there is sufficient room to complete your manoeuvre safely and smoothly.

No U-turn

(See Section 9 for rules/guidelines on turning)

Slowing down or stopping at the side of a road

○ Check in your mirror to make sure you can slow down and stop safely.

○ Signal your intention to change course and pull in.

○ Signal your intention to slow down either through the brake lights or by moving your right arm up and down outside your vehicle window (shown below) if you think your brake lights might not be seen or might not be working. If they are not working, have them repaired immediately.

- You **should** not leave your headlights on when stopping at the side of the road, including laybys or private property. If you need to leave your lights on, it is recommended that you use your 'side' or 'parking' lights only.

- Use a traffic lay-by if one is provided or pull in and stop close to the left-hand edge of the road.

Towing

If you are towing another vehicle or a trailer (including a boat trailer or a caravan), remember the following points.

- Make sure the tow bar or other towing device is strong enough and is attached securely so that it does not break or become loose when used.

- Make sure the breakaway brake/secondary coupling is in place and secured.

A 'breakaway brake' attached to a trailer is a braking device that can automatically stop the trailer if it becomes detached from the towing vehicle while moving. A 'secondary coupling' is usually a safety chain or wire rope or other similar connection which ensures the trailer stays attached to its towing vehicle if the main coupling fails or becomes detached. A secondary coupling is not needed if the trailer is equipped with a breakaway brake. Further information on these devices is available on *www.rsa.ie*.

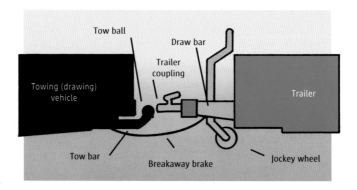

- Do not allow a distance of more than 4.5 metres (about 15 feet) between the vehicles or the vehicle and the trailer.

- If more than 1.5 metres separates the vehicles, use some warning device such as a white flag of at least 30 centimetres squared to draw attention to the tow bar.

- If towing a vehicle that has its own steering gear, make sure somebody remains in that vehicle to take charge of the steering.

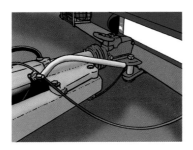

- If towing a vehicle, the person who steers the towed vehicle must hold a licence to drive the same category of vehicle.

- Make sure a trailer is fitted with brakes if it has a Maximum Authorised Mass (MAM) of more than 750kg or is more than half the laden weight of the drawing vehicle (whichever is lower). This includes a parking brake and a breakaway brake. Older trailers that don't have a breakaway brake must have a secondary coupling (a chain or wire rope) fitted instead.

- A combination of vehicles or an articulated vehicle more than 13 metres long must display a 'LONG VEHICLE' sign or signs on the back of the last trailer.

- You must mark any loads sticking out more than 1 metre from the back of the trailer with a red flag or marker board during the day. If you are towing this type of load at night, mark it with a red reflector and red lights.

- If the load is sticking out to the side and you are towing it at night, mark it with a light or lights showing a white light to the front and a red light to the back.

Loads must be safely distributed and securely tied down. You **should** avoid carrying loads that extend over the side of the trailer while it's being towed. Loads may extend over the side and rear of trailers provided the following limits are not exceeded:

- Loads (other than poles intended for use by telephone or electricity services) must not project more than 3 metres beyond the rearmost part of a trailer.

- Loads overhanging to the rear by more than 1 metre must be marked during the day with a red flag or cloth which is at least 300 millimetres square (about 12 inches square). However, at night time, overhanging loads must be fitted with a red reflector and a red light.

- Loads (other than loose agricultural produce which is not baled or in crates) must not project more than 300 millimetres (about 12 inches square) over the outermost point of the side of the trailer. At night time, these loads must be fitted with lights showing a white light to the front and a red light to the rear. These lights must be placed as close as possible to the outermost point of the load.

- If possible, loads should be evenly distributed across the trailer and positioned in such a way as to keep the nose weight (that is, the weight exerted by the trailer drawbar on the coupling) within the recommended limits for the drawing vehicle. Consult the owner's handbook for further details. If you have to carry a load that cannot be evenly distributed, make sure it is properly restrained and that individual axles or the drawbar are not overloaded. You might have to reduce the overall load to achieve this.

- When towing a trailer, the maximum speed at which the vehicle can travel may be different from the posted speed limit. Please see page 114 for more information.

Further information on towing different loads safely is available on *www.rsa.ie*.

Driving at night

Make sure your lights, indicators, reflectors and number plate lighting are clean and in good working order so that you can see clearly and be seen at all times. A clean windscreen is also important when driving at night.

You must drive at a speed that allows you to stop within the distance covered by your lights. Assuming good driving conditions on an unlit road, the headlights of a typical car let you see for about 100 metres. Dipped lights will let you see for about 30 metres and a car travelling at 100km/h will cover this distance in about a second.

Keep your headlights adjusted properly. If they are out of line, they are less effective and may dazzle oncoming traffic, even when dipped.

Even with the best headlights, you can see less at night than during the day. Pedestrians and unlit bicycles are extremely difficult to see in the dark, particularly if you have to deal with the glare of oncoming lights.

Some junctions are marked with special coloured studs and/or delineator posts to help road users determine where a junction is as they approach it at night or during periods of poor visibility.

Junction delineator post

Daytime running lights

'Daytime running lights' refers to driving with dipped headlights during daytime. The use of dipped headlights can help reduce the number of deaths and serious injuries on our roads.

If your vehicle is not fitted with daytime running lights, it is advisable to drive with your dipped headlights on during the daytime.

When to use headlights

If conditions require you to use headlights to drive safely, you **must** use them. Use dipped headlights at night or main beam headlights as appropriate. When in doubt, turn them on. Make sure that the red lights and number plate lighting at the back of your vehicle are working.

Use **dipped headlights**:

- just after the beginning (dusk) and before the end (dawn) of lighting-up hours;
- as long as they are needed to let you see clearly;
- when stopped in traffic;
- when meeting other traffic;
- in built-up areas where there is good street lighting;
- on continuously lit roads outside built-up areas;
- when following behind another vehicle;
- where there is dense fog, falling snow or heavy rain;
- when daylight is fading; and
- generally to avoid inconveniencing other traffic.

It is good practice to use dipped headlights or dim/dip lights, where fitted, instead of only sidelights in built-up areas where there is good street lighting.

- Use main beam headlights in situations, places and times outside of those listed above.
- Use fog lights only during dense fog and falling snow. You **must** turn them off at all other times.
- It is recommended that, if stopped (other than in traffic), you do not leave your headlights on and switch to your 'side' or 'parking' lights instead. You **should** not leave headlights on when parked.

What to do if you are dazzled by another vehicle's headlights

- Slow down and stop if necessary.
- Always watch for pedestrians or cyclists on your side of the road.
- If the dazzle is from an oncoming vehicle, avoid it by looking towards the verge (edge of your side of the road) until the vehicle has passed. If the dazzle is from a vehicle behind you and reflected in your mirror, operate the night-driving mode on the mirror.

Driving carefully behind other vehicles

Section 8 covers the importance of keeping a safe distance behind vehicles in front of you. In particular, don't drive on the tail lights of the vehicle in front. It gives a false sense of security and may lure you into driving too close or too fast, or both. If you see red vehicle lights in front of you, dip your headlights to avoid dazzling the driver of the vehicle ahead.

Using a horn

Only use a horn to:

○ warn other road users of on-coming danger; or

○ make them aware of your presence for safety reasons when reasonably necessary.

Remember, the horn does not give you the right of way.

Do not use a horn in a built-up area between 23.30hrs and 07.00hrs unless there is a traffic emergency.

> ### REMEMBER
>
> **You must drive having due regard to other road users.**

Section 6:

Traffic signs and road markings

///

You **must** know what traffic signs and road markings mean before you attempt
to drive on a public road. This section focuses on the signs that you as a driver
will come across most often. Sections 21 to 25 covers a range of the most
important signs currently used on Irish roads.

You **must** know and understand these signs and respond correctly when you see
them on the road.

Traffic signs and roadway markings are divided into three broad categories:

- Regulatory,
- Warning, and
- Information.

Sometimes signs from different categories are used together to improve road
safety.

Different types of signs are used for bus and cycle lanes, motorways and
railway crossings and bridges. There is also a special series of warning signs for
roadworks. These are all outlined at the end of this section.

Regulatory signs

These indicate what you **must** do under road traffic law, so all road users **must**
obey them. Regulatory signs are divided into a number of groups:

- Upright signs;
- Road markings; and
- Traffic lights.

This section concentrates on regulatory upright signs and road markings.
Section 7 covers traffic lights in detail.

Upright signs

What they look like:

These generally come in two formats. Their shape can be circular, octagonal, triangular or rectangular, as shown in the examples below:

- a white background with a red border and black letters, symbols or numbers, and

- a blue background with white symbols or letters.

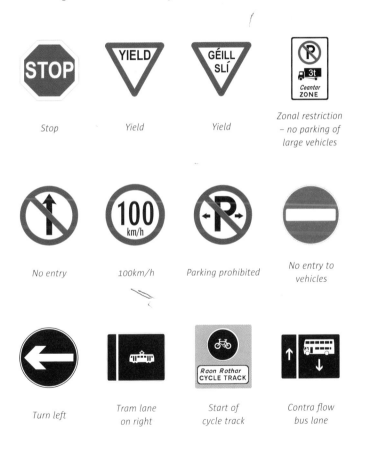

Stop	Yield	Yield	Zonal restriction – no parking of large vehicles
No entry	100km/h	Parking prohibited	No entry to vehicles
Turn left	Tram lane on right	Start of cycle track	Contra flow bus lane

Please note that it is a fixed charge offence of €60 to ignore the 'No entry to vehicles' sign pictured above.

The sign below applies to drivers of HGVs and large non-passenger vehicles. It means that vehicles with the number of axles shown (or more) cannot use the road during the times shown without a permit. You **should** check the information plate and/or the permit to confirm the time limits and any restrictions that apply.

No entry to goods vehicles (by reference to number of axles)

Information plate

The signs below apply to all drivers of vehicles which may exceed the applicable weight, width or length restrictions on certain roads. You **must** comply with such signs. It is an offence to proceed past such signs where your vehicle exceeds the applicable weight, width or length. This offence attracts a fixed charge of €60.

maximum width sign

maximum height sign

maximum design gross vehicle weight sign (safety)

maximum axle loading weight sign

Stop and Yield signs

As you can see from the diagram, the upright **Stop** sign is a red octagon with a white border. It is the only regulatory sign of this shape. Stop signs appear at junctions with major roads. If you approach a Stop sign, you must stop completely before entering the major road, no matter how quiet it might appear.

Stop

The upright **Yield** sign shown is just one version of this sign. Other versions are the same shape and colour but might say 'Yield Right of Way', or 'Géill Slí'. If you see a Yield sign on the road, usually near a junction or roundabout, you must give way to any traffic on a major road ahead and you must not proceed onto the main road until it is safe to do so. Make sure you allow enough time to complete your manoeuvre. It is better to be safe than sorry.

Yield   *Géill Slí*

Traffic lane control signs

These traffic lane control signs will be found on **national roads or motorways**. When the signs are operational, the amber lights at the top and bottom will flash in turn.

A green arrow pointing down means the lane is open and you can proceed in that lane.

Go (lane open)

A red X means the lane is closed. You **must** stop. You **must not** pass this sign. It has the same effect as a stop sign.

Stop (lane closed)

A green arrow pointing to the left means you **must** move into the left-hand lane. In doing so you **must** observe the general rules of the road relating to safely changing lanes.

Move into the left-hand lane

A green arrow pointing to the right means you **must** move into the right-hand lane. In doing so you **must** observe the general rules of the road relating to safely changing lanes.

Move into the right-hand lane

Where a driver proceeds beyond one of the above traffic lane control signs other than in accordance with the sign or without yielding, they will be liable for a fixed charge of €60.

One-way streets

When you are approaching a one-way street, you may see one of two regulatory signs. If you are at the entrance to a one-way street, you will see the 'Proceed Straight Ahead' regulatory sign. If you are approaching the 'wrong' end of a one-way street, you will see the regulatory road markings shown below to indicate 'No Entry' and you must not enter past those markings.

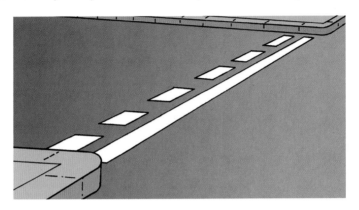

You may also see an upright 'No Entry' sign with the road markings.

Straight ahead　　　*No entry*　　*No entry to vehicles*

Driving in a one-way street

Even though all traffic on a one-way street is travelling in the same direction, you **should** still drive on the left-hand side. You may leave the left-hand side only if you intend to overtake or turn right up ahead. You may drive on either side of a traffic island, but take note of arrow markings on the road.

Only change lanes if you have to. If you have to change lanes, check your mirrors and blind spots for any traffic coming up behind you or overtaking you. When the way is clear, signal your intention and move, giving way to any traffic already in the lane.

When turning right from a one-way street, drive as close as you can to the right-hand side.

Remember that the road at the end of a one-way street may be two-way. You may see the warning sign below if it is.

Two-way traffic

Streets for pedestrians

The regulatory sign below shows that the street is closed to all road users except pedestrians at the time shown on the information plate underneath.

Pedestrianised

street

Road markings

Road markings are a traffic sign in the form and design of a marking on the surface of the road. They have the same status as upright signs. Road users must obey these road markings.

The diagrams below show the most common types of road marking and what they mean.

Road markings	What they mean	
Single or double continuous white lines along the centre of the road	All traffic must keep to the left of the line (except in an emergency or for access).	
Longer white lines / warning lines along the centre of the road	These warning lines alert drivers to hazards such as restricted vision, approach to a junction, approach to a roundabout, a hill, crests, bends and continuous white line ahead.	
Short broken white lines along the centre of the road	These divide two lanes of traffic travelling in opposite directions. You must not cross them unless it is safe to do so.	
Double broken white lines along the centre of the road	These alert drivers to continuous white lines a short distance ahead. As a driver, you must not cross them unless it is safe to do so.	
A broken white line with a single white line along the centre of the road	The driver must obey the line that is nearest to them. In this picture, the driver in the car must remain to the left of the continuous white line.	
A single broken yellow line along the side of the road	This road contains a hard shoulder, which is normally **only** for pedestrians and cyclists. If a driver wants to allow a vehicle behind them to overtake, they may pull in to the hard shoulder briefly as long as no pedestrians or cyclists are already using it and no junctions or entrances are nearby. Different rules exist for hard shoulders on motorways. See Section 11 for details.	

Road markings	What they mean	
A broken white Yield line crossing the left-hand lane. A white triangular Yield symbol may also be provided with the Yield line.	The driver must give right-of-way to any traffic on a major road ahead. The yield line usually appears with an upright Yield sign.	
A continuous white Stop line crossing the left-hand lane. The word STOP may also be provided with the Stop line.	The driver must come to a complete stop before entering a major road. The stop line sometimes appears with an upright Stop sign.	
An advanced stop line for cyclists, which is in front of the stop line for other traffic	Cyclists may position themselves in front of other traffic at a junction controlled by traffic lights. The motor vehicle driver must wait behind the first white line they reach and not cross into the shaded area. The driver must also give cyclists enough time and space to move off when the lights turn green.	
A turning box showing a white arrow in a white edged box, found at junctions controlled by traffic lights	This shows where to position a vehicle if you want to take a right turn. Do not proceed into the box through a red light. If oncoming traffic means you cannot take a right turn immediately, you must wait in the box until you can safely take the turn.	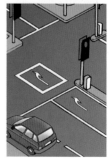

Warning signs

These signs warn you of hazards ahead, such as roundabouts, crossroads, dangerous bends or anything else that would call on you to drive more carefully. You **should** always take special care when you see a warning sign. If you fail to observe these signs, you could create an emergency.

What they look like

All warning signs have the same format. They:

- are diamond or rectangular in shape;

- have a yellow background with a black border; and

- use a black symbol to show the hazard ahead.

They are also upright, meaning they are at the side of the road or mounted on a wall instead of painted onto the road surface.

This diagram shows some of the most common warning signs.

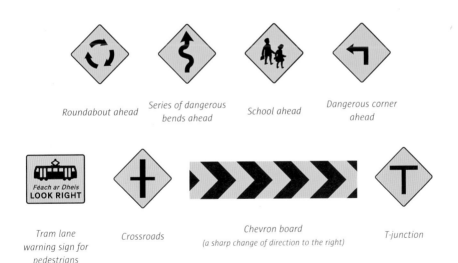

Roundabout ahead

Series of dangerous bends ahead

School ahead

Dangerous corner ahead

Tram lane warning sign for pedestrians

Crossroads

Chevron board
(a sharp change of direction to the right)

T-junction

Section 22 has more examples of warning signs.

Roadwork signs

These signs differ from other warning signs. You **should** always take extra care and reduce your speed when you see these signs.

The signs are:

- ○ rectangular or diamond in shape; and

- ○ orange with a black border and black symbols or words.

The images below are examples of these signs.

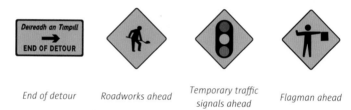

| End of detour | Roadworks ahead | Temporary traffic signals ahead | Flagman ahead |

The movement of vehicles at or near roadworks is controlled by law.

Stop and Go traffic control at roadworks

When roadworks are being carried out you **must** stop when you see the Stop sign (pictured below). You may only proceed through or past the roadworks when the Go sign (Téigh) is displayed. It is an offence not to obey these signs.

Where plant or machinery is crossing the roadway and no matter what direction you approach from, you **must** stop when you see the Stop sign (pictured below). You **must** obey these road signs. The signs can be operated by mechanical or manual means.

Manual traffic control sign at roadworks

Stop   Either form of Go or Téigh can be used

There are more signs displayed in Section 23.

Variable Message Signs (VMS)

These signs provide information in an electronic format and are designed to inform you of a range of issues relating to roads, roadworks and road safety. The content of the sign will change, depending on the situation. You **should** pay particular attention to these signs and messages.

Information regarding speed limit

New road layout ahead

Mobile VMS (displaying text message)

Mobile VMS (displaying chevrons)

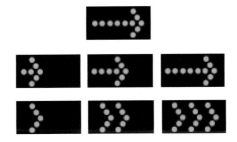

Arrow formats for mobile VMS

Information signs

As their name suggests, these signs give information about directions and distances from your current location.

What they look like

There are three formats for information signs:

- blue signs with white letters on motorways,
- green signs with white letters, which are on national roads, and
- white signs with black letters, which are on local and regional roads.

Advanced direction signs

| Motorway | National road | National road | Regional road |

Motorway information signs

All motorway signs are blue. The following table identifies the most common signs and what they mean.

Motorway signs		What they mean
	Motorway ahead	There is an entrance to a motorway ahead and the road users listed on the sign must not enter the motorway.
	Entry to motorway	The road user is now entering a motorway and must obey motorway rules. This sign usually appears beside the 'Motorway ahead' sign.
	Countdown sign	The driver is 300 metres from the next exit off the motorway.
	Countdown sign	The driver is 200 metres from the next exit.
	Countdown sign	The driver is 100 metres from the next exit.
	Motorway ends 500m ahead	There are 500 metres to the end of the motorway.
	End of motorway	The driver has reached the end of the motorway.
	Lane gain sign	An additional lane is joining the motorway.
	Next exit sign	Indicates distance to the next exit and supplementary routes.

Section 11 covers the main rules on motorway driving. It is an offence to disobey these rules.

Markings for merging and diverging traffic (hatched markings)

The diagrams show how the markings can be used for:

○ merging traffic – for example, where two lanes of traffic become one, and

○ diverging traffic – for example, where channelling traffic taking a left turn away from traffic going straight ahead.

Markings for separating traffic (hatched markings)

Hatched markings can also be used for separating traffic travelling in opposite directions (in what are called central median islands).

If you see these markings on a road, you **must not** enter the area they cover.

A 2-plus-1 road consists of two lanes in one direction of travel and one lane in the other direction. The two-lane section allows for safe overtaking and alternates with a one-lane section roughly every 2 kilometres.

There may be a safety barrier in the centre of the road which separates the two directions of traffic and prevents drivers from overtaking in the one-lane section. If vehicles need to turn right, they can do so at junctions.

In other cases, vehicles that need to turn right or turn around may first turn left onto a minor road and perform a U-turn in the area provided for that purpose. They can then resume their journey as originally intended.

A form of 2-plus-1 road already exists on some climbing lanes on national primary roads – the uphill stretch is two lanes and the downhill stretch is just one.

Traffic calming signs

Some towns and villages use road features, signs and markings for traffic calming, which generally involves slowing the pace of traffic and managing its flow at junctions. The type of signs used for traffic calming are regulatory, warning and information. When you enter one of these towns or villages, you will see an information sign that may be combined with the town or village name and a speed limit sign.

In these towns, expect the following speed reducing measures:

- ○ traffic islands,

- ○ gateways,

- ○ mini-roundabouts,

- ○ build-outs,

- ○ chicanes, and

- ○ pinch points.

You may also come across the following signs on residential roads in built-up areas. These signs indicate that the road includes ramps, speed cushions or speed tables.

Ramps on road   Mini-Roundabout ahead   Traffic calming   Slow Zone

Please note that it is a fixed-charge offence of €60 to violate the rules relating to mini-roundabouts, the information sign for which is shown above.

Urban slow zones (30Km/h) for housing estates

Slow zones are usually found in self-contained areas with local roads and low traffic volumes. Slow zones are usually accompanied by other traffic calming measures such as speed bumps. Road users **should** take extra care and expect the unexpected.

Special signs and markings for buses, trams, rail and light rail

There are special regulatory signs and markings used to show the parts of a road that are reserved for particular vehicles – namely buses, bicycles, trams and light rail. The signs can be regulatory, warning and/or information signs. The design of these signs is consistent with the design of regulatory, warning and/ or information signs.

This section deals with the more common signs that you will see as a road user. You **should** take care when you see any signs for buses, bicycles, trams, rail and light rail.

Bus signs

Bus lanes

Bus lanes are sections of road reserved for buses, whether public or private. Taxis and bicycles may also use some bus lanes.

Where there is a bus lane, you will see an upright blue and white sign on the side of the road on a pole, and on the roadway there will be markings of a continuous white line and the words 'Lána Bus'. You **must** obey the road marking and the sign. The white plate shows when the section of road is meant only for the buses shown. Normally, bus lanes operate from 7am to 7pm or during peak hours. Outside these times, all traffic may use them. You **should** check the information plate to confirm the time limits that apply.

There are two types of bus lane:

- with-flow, and
- contra-flow.

With-flow bus lane

Contra-flow bus lane

A with-flow near-side bus lane, shown below, runs in the same direction as the traffic beside it. It can be used by bicycles and taxis as well as buses, and is normally reserved during the periods shown on information signs at the start of the lane.

Advance information sign for with-flow bus lane

With-flow bus lane on left (near-side)

Advance information sign for off-side bus lane

With-flow bus lane on right (off-side)

Information plate

Contra-flow bus lane

A contra-flow bus lane runs in the opposite direction to the traffic beside it. It is reserved only for buses, which generally means that no other traffic may use it, day or night, unless signs authorise its use by cyclists.

Contra-flow bus lane

If a 'Yield' sign appears at the end of the bus lane, the bus **must** give way to other vehicles as it merges back into normal traffic.

Bus-only streets

As their name suggests, these streets are intended only for buses. Other traffic may use them only to get access to a building or side road.

Bus only street

Section 10 covers the rules on parking in bus lanes.

Trams/light rail signs

Road users **must** be familiar with signs for tram tracks for on-street trams (such as the Luas in Dublin city and suburbs).

Regulatory signs for tram lanes

The blue signs pictured below show that a tram lane is running beside a traffic lane ahead. A driver can only enter the tram lane to overtake another vehicle when it is safe to do so.

Tram lane on left   *Tram lane on right*

The red and white sign pictured below shows that a pedestrian may not walk beyond the point where the sign is placed.

No entry for pedestrians to tramway

A 'No Entry' sign with the information plate 'Except Trams – Ach amháin Tramanna' means that the street is only for trams and no other traffic is allowed enter it.

Tram only street   *Tram and access only street*

A 'No Entry' sign with the information plate 'Except Trams and Access – Ach amháin Tramanna agus Rochtain' means that a driver or cyclist may enter the street if they need to enter or leave a building.

Remember, when approaching junctions where there is a tram line:

- obey traffic lights, and

- keep yellow junction boxes completely clear.

For more information on traffic lights, see Section 7. For more information on types of junctions, see Section 9.

Warning signs for tram lanes

Pedestrians **should** cross tram tracks only where they see the sign pictured below. It displays a tram symbol and the words 'Féach gach treo - LOOK BOTH WAYS' to indicate a tramway crossing point.

The alternative text that may be shown on this warning is 'Féach ar dheis, LOOK RIGHT' or 'Féach ar chlé, LOOK LEFT'.

Look both ways   *Look right*   *Look left*

When in the vicinity of tramways, pedestrians are advised to:

- stop, look both ways, listen;

- walk, do not run;

- always use designated crossing points; and

- obey signs and listen for warning horns and tram chimes.

Cyclists need to take special care because tram tracks can be slippery, especially during wet or icy weather. The Luas warning sign for cyclists is shown below.

Slippery for cyclists

In particular, cyclists **should** avoid braking while on tram rails. They **should** always cross tram rails at a right angle or as close to it as possible.

They **should** take care to avoid getting their bicycle wheels caught in the groove of the tram rails.

Road users **should** be aware of the overhead wires used by trams. This is particularly important for drivers carrying loads and people carrying long items. All road users **should** be careful not to risk electrocution by touching overhead wires, even indirectly.

The LÁNA TRAM roadmarking sign may be used to draw attention to the

Overhead electric cables   *Tramway crossing ahead*   *Lána tram road marking*

presence of tram tracks. It is an information sign to tell you there is a section of road used by trams and vehicles. You **should** be aware that trams are controlled by a different type of light signal and that you need to be extra careful.

tram proceed   *tram stop*

Drivers must not follow a tram through a traffic light controlled junction unless permitted to do so.

Railway level crossings

Introduction

A railway level crossing is an intersection where a road or passage crosses a railway track.

Drivers and other users **should** be aware of the different types of crossing, and **should** know how to cross safely. You **must** always approach a level crossing with care.

This section outlines the different types of level crossings and the correct and safe way to use them.

As you approach any railway level crossing you **must** obey the signs and roadway markings, slow down and be prepared to stop.

You **must not** enter a yellow box area unless you can clear it without stopping. You **must** never stop on the railway tracks.

At unattended level crossings:

Use the **Rail Cross Code** each time you cross:

- ⊙ **Always expect a train**
- ⊙ **Stop, Look and Listen**
  - • **Stop** – at least two metres before the railway line
  - • **Look** – right and left, watching for the lights of approaching trains
  - • **Listen** – for a train horn or whistle
- ⊙ **Give Way to Trains**

  Let any approaching train pass, then **look** right and left again
- ⊙ **When the railway is clear, cross quickly**.

REMEMBER

Never stop a vehicle on the railway tracks.

Emergency actions at level crossings

If your vehicle stalls or an animal strays on the railway:

- Move everyone well clear of the railway.

- Leave the animal or vehicle where it is.

- Tell the railway controller, using the phone number displayed at the crossing.

- State the 'crossing number' shown at the crossing.

This identification number is different for each level crossing

CROSSING NUMBER

XC 123

Iarnród Éireann

Example 'crossing number' plate shown at a level crossing

Unusual movements across level crossings

Drivers of very high vehicles should note that at level crossings with overhead electrified lines, such as on the DART network, the safe headroom is 5 metres (16ft 4ins).

You **should** contact the railway in advance, using the phone number displayed at the level crossing, when arranging special events such as matches, funerals or processions that will involve the use of the level crossing.

In addition, at level crossings with iron gates or automatic half-barriers, or on minor roads where protection is by traffic lights only, you **should** contact the railway, using the phone number displayed at the level crossing, to get permission before crossing with:

- awkward vehicles – for example, long, low, wide, heavy or slow, vehicles

- vehicles carrying dangerous goods or exceptional loads

- crowds of people or herds of animals

General instructions for the safe use of different types of level crossing

1. Unattended railway level crossings with iron gates

These unattended level crossings are found on minor roads. The railway is normally guarded by iron gates which must be kept shut – there is no other protection. The user has the responsibility to open and shut the gates.

These crossings can be dangerous to use and drivers **should** use all available help to cross safely. It is preferable for drivers to use a bridge or an attended or automated level crossing where one is available.

*Level crossing ahead, guarded
by gates or lifting barrier*

Drivers – what you should do:

Prepare

- STOP clear of the gates.
- Switch off phone and music systems.
- Open windows on driver and passenger sides.
- Read instructions at the crossing.
- Get a helper to operate the gates if possible.

Use the **Rail Cross Code** each time you cross:

- **Always expect a train**
- **Stop, Look and Listen**
  - **Stop** – at least two metres before the railway line
  - **Look** – right and left, watching for the lights of approaching trains
  - **Listen** – for a train horn or whistle
- **Give Way to Trains**

  Let any approaching train pass, then **look** right and left again
- **When the railway is clear, cross quickly**.

Drive across safely

- First walk across and open both gates.
- Drive forward and STOP two metres clear of the railway line.
- Apply your handbrake.
- Look right and left and listen.
- Drive across quickly when the railway is clear.
- Stop well clear of the tracks on the opposite side.

Drivers – what you must do:

Shut gates at unattended level crossings

- You must shut and fasten the gates as soon as you and any person, animal or vehicle under your care has passed through.
- Even if the gates are open when you arrive, you must shut and fasten them after you to protect others.
- Failure to shut and fasten the gates is an offence.

> ## REMEMBER
>
> **Stay Alert...**
>
> **STOP, LOOK and LISTEN**
>
> **Give way to trains**
>
> **Always shut and fasten the iron gates**
>
> **Failure to do so is an offence.**

2. *Attended railway level crossings with gates or barriers operated by railway staff*

These level crossings are manually operated by railway staff. The level crossing is only open to the public when the gates are fully open to the road.

Level crossing ahead,
guarded by gates or
lifting barrier

Drivers – what you must do:

- ○ Slow down approaching the crossing.
- ○ Be prepared to stop if necessary.

3. Automated railway level crossings protected by road traffic lights only

These level crossings have no barriers or gates. Users must obey the road traffic lights at these open level crossings.

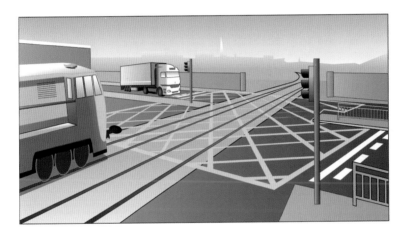

*Level crossing ahead,
unguarded by gates or
lifting barrier*

Drivers – what you must do:

- ○ Obey the rules for traffic lights.
- ○ If you have already entered the crossing, move clear as quickly as possible.

4. Automated railway level crossings with barriers and flashing red lights

These level crossings have barriers which automatically come down when a train is approaching. The amber light is the same as an amber traffic light – stop safely when the amber light shows. Flashing red lights have the same meaning as a steady red traffic light – stop safely when they show.

Level crossing ahead with lights and barriers. Crossing may also have audible warning alarms.

Drivers – what you must do:

- Obey the rules for traffic lights.

- If you have already entered the crossing, move clear as quickly as possible.

- Wait for all lights to go out and barriers to be raised before moving on.

REMEMBER

A flashing red light always means stop

You should never zigzag around the barriers of a level crossing

Pedestrians crossing the railway

Pedestrians – what you should do:

Prepare

- Switch off phones and music systems.

- Read any instructions at the crossing.

- Contact the railway in advance, using the phone number displayed at the level crossing:

  - if you are arranging special events such as matches, funerals or processions that will involve the use of the level crossing

  - to get permission before crossing the railway with crowds of people or herds of animals at a level crossing with iron gates or automatic half-barriers, or on minor roads where protection is by traffic lights only

- Take extra care with a wheelchair, pram or buggy.

Beware

- Never trespass onto a railway line.

- Always expect a train.

- Supervise children near the railway.

- Keep dogs on a lead.

- Only cross at a designated level crossing
- Obey traffic lights, where provided
- If crossing with a pram, wheelchair or bicycle, you should cross the tracks carefully to avoid getting the wheels caught in the groove.

Use the **Rail Cross Code** each time you cross:

- **Always expect a train**
- **Stop, Look and Listen**
  - **Stop** – at least two metres before the railway line
  - **Look** – right and left, watching for the lights of approaching trains
  - **Listen** – for a train horn or whistle
- **Give Way to Trains**

  Let any approaching train pass, then **look** right and left again
- **When the railway is clear, cross quickly**.

REMEMBER

STOP, LOOK and LISTEN

Give way to trains

Never trespass onto the railway

Pedestrians – what you must do:

Shut gates at unattended level crossings

- You must shut and fasten the gates as soon as you and any person, animal or vehicle under your care has passed through.
- Even if the gates are open when you arrive, you must shut and fasten them after you to protect others.
- Failure to shut and fasten the gates is an offence.

> ### REMEMBER
>
> **Always shut and fasten the iron gates.**
>
> **Failure to do so is an offence.**

Emergency actions at level crossings

If your vehicle stalls or an animal strays on the railway:

- Move everyone well clear of the railway.

- Leave the animal or vehicle where it is.

- Tell the railway controller, using the phone number displayed at the crossing.

- State the 'crossing number' shown at the crossing.

Example 'Crossing number' plate displayed at a level crossing

Cyclists and horse riders crossing the railway

- As you approach a level crossing, you **must** obey the signs, slow down and be prepared to stop.

- You **must** obey the Rules of the Road.

- Follow the relevant instructions and emergency actions applying to pedestrians at railway level crossings.

- Cyclists – cross at right angles to the tracks or else dismount to avoid getting the wheels caught in the groove.

- Cyclists and horse riders – dismount and walk across the railway line at iron-gated level crossings and at passages.

Railway bridges and overhead structures

Introduction

A railway bridge is a structure where a road or passage crosses a railway track by a bridge either under or over the railway. As you approach a railway bridge, you **must** obey any signs and roadway markings.

You will see an information notice similar to the one shown below on railway bridges. This sign plate gives an identification number for the bridge and Iarnród Éireann's emergency contact phone number.

This bridge identification number is different for each railway bridge

OBWW 123
If this bridge is struck by a vehicle please telephone Iarnród Éireann
(01) 8555 454

Example Railway Bridge Identification Plate

Emergency actions – reporting bridge incidents

You **must** report immediately any incident of your vehicle striking a railway bridge or structure whether or not damage is obvious. Drivers **must** use the emergency telephone number to contact Iarnród Eireann following any incident at a bridge, stating the nature of the incident and the bridge identification number given on the sign.

If you cannot make contact immediately at this number, you **must** immediately notify a member of An Garda Síochána.

> REMEMBER
>
> **You must report any incident of your vehicle impacting a railway structure.**
>
> **Failure to do so is an offence.**

Bridge under the railway with height restriction

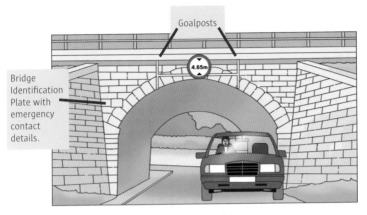

This is an example of a bridge with a height restriction under the railway. The sign below is a regulatory height restriction sign, which may appear on a height-restricted railway bridge. You **must not** pass unless your vehicle is lower than the height shown on the sign.

Height restriction

In the case of arch bridges, the indicated height is available only over a certain width of the arch. This width is shown by 'goalposts'.

As you approach a bridge under the railway, you may see an advance warning sign such as the 'restricted headroom' sign below showing the height restriction that applies at the bridge. The height restriction is written first in feet and inches and then in metres.

Low bridge ahead
(restricted headroom)

Your vehicle, including any load being carried, must be lower than the height shown on the warning sign. It is very important to know the height of your vehicle and of any load being carried before you start your journey.

You may also encounter advance information signs with warnings such as the signs below.

 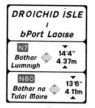

Advance information sign for low clearance railway bridge

REMEMBER

Know your height. Know your route.

Bridge over the railway

This is an example of a bridge over the railway. There can be restrictions on vehicles entitled to use these bridges. These restrictions will usually be related to vehicle weight, width and number of axles.

These are some of the signs that you may see at a bridge over a railway.

As you approach a railway bridge you **must** obey any road signs and roadway markings.

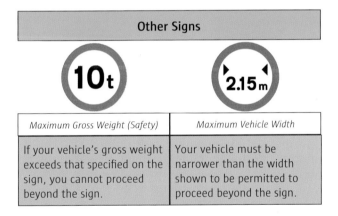

Examples of Weight Restriction signage	
Maximum Gross Weight	*Maximum Axle Weight*
The total weight of your vehicle including its load must weigh less than this to safely proceed beyond the sign.	If any axle on your vehicle exceeds this weight, you cannot proceed beyond the sign.

Other Signs	
Maximum Gross Weight (Safety)	*Maximum Vehicle Width*
If your vehicle's gross weight exceeds that specified on the sign, you cannot proceed beyond the sign.	Your vehicle must be narrower than the width shown to be permitted to proceed beyond the sign.

Road tunnel signs

These lane control signs are found above each traffic lane at, or on, the approach to the entrance to a road tunnel and at regular intervals inside a road tunnel. When the signs are operational, the amber lights at the top and bottom will flash in turn.

A **green** arrow pointing down means the lane is open and you are allowed to proceed in that lane.

Go (lane open)

A **red** X means the lane is closed. You **must** stop. You **must not** pass this sign. It has the same effect as a stop sign.

Stop (lane closed)

A **green** arrow pointing to the left means you **must** move into the left-hand lane. In doing so you **must** observe the general rules of the road relating to safely changing lanes.

Move into the left-hand lane

A **green** arrow pointing to the right means you **must** move into the right-hand lane. In doing so you **must** observe the general rules of the road relating to safely changing lanes.

Move into the right-hand lane

The following sign means that goods vehicles and large non-passenger vehicles with three or more axles cannot use the right-hand lane of the carriageway. You **must** travel in the left-hand lane of the carriageways in a road tunnel.

*In a tunnel, goods vehicles cannot use right-hand
lane (by reference to number of axles)*

The regulation does not apply when:

- a **red** X is displayed over the left-hand lane, which means the lane **must not** be used;

- a **green** arrow is displayed over the right-hand lane, which directs all vehicles to use the right-hand lane; or

- the left-hand lane is blocked.

There are two forms of speed limit signs in tunnels.

- A standard speed limit sign applies where there is a fixed speed limit in a tunnel. You **must** obey the speed limit and remember this is the maximum permitted speed, not the required speed.

30km/h	*40km/h*	*50km/h*	*60km/h*	*80km/h*

- Where the speed limit can vary in a tunnel, you will see a variable message sign, which is a black square with a red circle and numbers in white or yellow. The speed limit is shown by the numbers and will vary according to traffic conditions and road safety considerations. You **must** obey the speed limit and remember this is the maximum permitted speed, not the required speed.

30km/h	*40km/h*	*50km/h*	*60km/h*	*80km/h*

Section 7:
Traffic lights and signals

///

This section builds on Section 6, which covers traffic signs and road markings. This section covers two general forms of traffic signals:

- ○ traffic lights, which direct the flow of traffic, and
- ○ signals given by motorists and cyclists to indicate their intent.

Traffic lights

These include lights controlling junctions and pedestrian crossings.

A red light means 'Stop'. If the light is red as you approach it, you **must not** go beyond the stop line at that light or, if there is no stop line, you **must not** go beyond the light.

A green light means you may go on if the way is clear. Take special care if you intend to turn left or right and give way to pedestrians who are crossing. A green light is not a right of way – it is an indication that you can proceed with caution.

REMEMBER

A green light is not a right of way, it is an indication that you may proceed with caution, but only if the way is clear.

An amber light means that you **must not** go beyond the stop line or, if there is no stop line, you **must not** go beyond the light. However, you may go on if you are so close to the line or the light when the amber light first appears that stopping would be dangerous.

A green arrow (also known as a filter light) means that you may move on in the direction of the arrow, assuming it is safe and the way is clear, even if a red light is also showing.

If you wish to turn right at a set of traffic lights that has an arrow to the right, drive into the junction when you see a green light, taking care not to block any oncoming traffic. Then, when it is safe, finish your turn. You **should** only wait for the filter arrow for turning right when you are in the junction and if it would be dangerous to finish your turn before the filter light appears.

A flashing amber arrow pointing left can appear at a junction with another road. It means that you may move on past the traffic light, but only if you first give way to traffic already coming through the junction on the other road.

Remember that a flashing amber light at a pelican crossing means you **must** yield to pedestrians. See Section 18, on pedestrian lights.

REMEMBER

You should always approach traffic lights at a speed that will allow you to stop if the amber light appears.

Cycle track lights

- A red light showing a figure of a cyclist means that the cyclist **must** stop at the traffic light.

- A green light showing a figure of a cyclist means the cyclist may move beyond the light as long as this does not put other road users in danger.

- A flashing green light or an amber light showing a figure of a cyclist means the cyclist may not cross the road unless they had started crossing when there was a steady green cyclist light.

REMEMBER

Cyclists – you must obey the traffic lights and may only proceed past a green traffic light if it is safe to do so.

Signals by motorists and cyclists

A motorist **must** always signal **before** they change their course. This means signalling clearly and in good time before:

- moving off,
- turning right or left,
- changing lanes,
- overtaking,
- slowing down, or
- stopping.

Signalling

Signals are an indication of intent – they do not confer a right of way. The law requires you to signal your intention of what you are doing on the road. This means signalling properly before moving off, turning right or left, changing lanes, overtaking, slowing down or stopping. You must signal clearly and in good time.

If you are concerned that, for whatever reason, your direction indicators or stop lamps are not giving an adequate signal, use clear, decisive hand signals as well.

An indicator is not a right of way.

Before you start to manoeuvre, you must exercise due care and attention with particular heed to other users of the road, prevailing road conditions and how your driving will impact other road users.

Always take care, especially when you:

- intend to change lane;

- turn across oncoming traffic;

- drive onto or exit from a roundabout; and

- drive into or reverse into a parking space.

Hand signals

Make sure you use hand signals to help, rather than confuse, other road users. Make sure you are familiar with the hand signals shown on the next two pages. Be prepared to use the appropriate hand signal where it will help others to understand your intentions.

Learner drivers should be guided by their approved driving instructor on when and where a hand signal might be particularly useful. For example:

- when turning right just after changing position to pass stationary traffic on the left; or

- to indicate to oncoming traffic that you intend to give way at a pedestrian crossing; or

- where you believe another road user may not be able to see your flashing indicators; or

- where you believe your indicators are not working (you should have them repaired before continuing your journey).

The signals for cyclists also apply to motorists and people in charge of horse-drawn vehicles and agricultural machinery not fitted with indicators.

The following are the hand signals to be used:

Hand signals to be given to traffic behind you

I am going to move out or turn to my right.

I am going to turn to my left.
Note that the car driver moves his arm and hand in an anti-clockwise direction.

I am going to slow down or stop.

Hand signals to be given to a pointsman and oncoming traffic

I want to turn right.

I want to turn left.
Note that the car driver points the
right forearm and hand with the
fingers extended to the left.

I want to go straight on.

I want to slow or stop.

The signals for the cyclist apply also to a motorcyclist and to a person in charge
of a horse-drawn vehicle.

REMEMBER

**Signals show only what you are intending to do – they never give you
right of way.**

Section 8:

Speed limits

//

A vehicle **must** not be driven at a speed exceeding that which will enable its driver to bring it to a halt within a distance the driver can see to be clear.

This section describes the rules for keeping pace in traffic and the speed limits that apply on different types of road and to different vehicles.

As a driver, you **must** always be aware of your speed and judge the appropriate speed for your vehicle, taking into account:

- ⊙ driving conditions;

- ⊙ other users of the road;

- ⊙ current weather conditions;

- ⊙ all possible hazards; and

- ⊙ speed limits.

Driving conditions relate to the volume of traffic around you and the quality of the road.

Other users of the road include motorcyclists, cyclists, pedestrians, school children, animals and all others you, as a driver, **should** expect to see on the road.

Possible hazards include anything you can see that could give rise to an emergency, such as oncoming traffic if you are turning onto a major road. They also include anything you cannot yet see and anything you can reasonably expect to happen, such as a pedestrian walking onto the road in front of you, a child running onto the road between parked cars, or animals on the roadway. It includes your own physical and mental state while driving (for example whether you are stressed or tired) and the condition of your vehicle.

Driving safely in traffic – the two-second rule

Your vehicle is your responsibility. You **must** be in control at all times.

You **must** keep your vehicle to a speed that allows you to stop it:

- safely, in a controlled way;

- on the correct side of the road;

- within the distance that you can see to be clear; and

- without risk or harm to you, your passengers and any other users of the road.

In traffic, the distance between your vehicle and the one in front of you is known as the 'safe headway'. Keep a safe headway by ensuring you are at least two seconds behind the vehicle in front. This is known as the 'two-second rule'. You can use the following steps to check if you are obeying the rule:

- On a dry road, choose a point like a lamp post or road sign.

- When the vehicle in front passes that point, say out loud, 'Only a fool breaks the two-second rule'.

- Check your position in relation to your chosen point as you finish saying this. If you have already passed the point, you are driving too close to the vehicle in front and need to pull back.

- In wet weather, double the distance between your vehicle and the one in front of you by saying 'Only a fool breaks the two-second rule' twice.

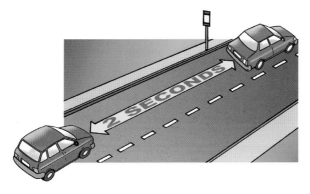

Use a fixed point to help measure a two-second gap.

> ## REMEMBER
>
> **Never drive closer than indicated by the two-second rule. If you drive too close to the vehicle in front (tailgating) and it brakes suddenly, you may not have enough time to react. If you run into the vehicle, you will be liable for any damage caused.**

Avoid driving too slowly

In normal road and traffic conditions, safely keep up with the pace of the traffic flow while obeying the speed limit. While you must keep a safe distance away from the vehicle in front, you should not drive so slowly that your vehicle unnecessarily blocks other road users. If you drive too slowly, you risk frustrating other drivers, which could lead to dangerous overtaking. However, remember: you must not drive at a speed at which you cannot stop the vehicle within the distance you can see to be clear ahead.

Speed limits

Signed speed limits set the maximum speed at which vehicles may legally travel on a section of road between speed limit signs, assuming the vehicles are not restricted in any way.

The signs indicate the maximum speed at which your vehicle may travel on a particular road or stretch of road, not the required speed for the road.

There are two types of speed limit:

- ◉ speed limits that apply to roads; and
- ◉ speed limits that apply to certain types of vehicles.

Speed limits on roads

All public roads have speed limits. In most cases, a 'default' speed limit applies. This automatically applies to a particular type of road if there is no speed limit sign to show otherwise.

The following table sets down the default speed limits for different roads under the Road Traffic Act 2004.

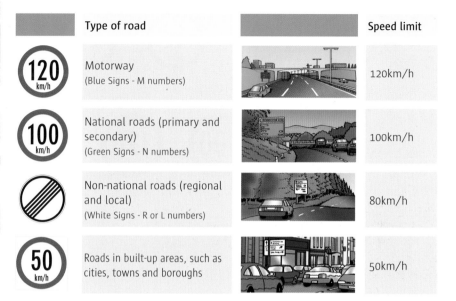

	Type of road		Speed limit
120 km/h	Motorway (Blue Signs - M numbers)		120km/h
100 km/h	National roads (primary and secondary) (Green Signs - N numbers)		100km/h
⊘	Non-national roads (regional and local) (White Signs - R or L numbers)		80km/h
50 km/h	Roads in built-up areas, such as cities, towns and boroughs		50km/h

Local authorities can apply special speed limits to roads, for example:

- at particular times, such as when children are entering or leaving schools (See Section 19);

- on different sides on a dual carriageway;

- at selected locations such as a tunnel, where the limit may be lowered if one lane **must** be closed;

- where there is a series of bends; and

- at roadworks.

If the local authority sets a special speed limit, you will see one of the signs below. Speed limit signs, like most other regulatory signs, have a red border, white background and black numbers and letters. They show the speed in kilometres per hour (km/h). (For more information on regulatory and other traffic signs, see Section 6.)

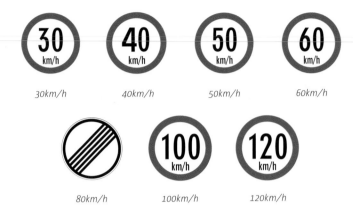

30km/h 40km/h 50km/h 60km/h

80km/h 100km/h 120km/h

The main speed limit signs on national primary and other roads are sometimes followed by small repeater signs to remind you of the road's speed limit.

No vehicle other than fire engines, ambulances or Garda vehicles may exceed the road speed limit at any time.

REMEMBER

The alternative design for the 80km/h speed limit sign, outlined above, may be provided:

- **on a local road to indicate that a speed limit of 80km/h applies; or**

- **at locations where the local authority has determined that this special speed limit applies.**

Periodic speed limits

Normally, speed limits apply 24 hours a day and all year round. In certain situations, local authorities can apply a special speed limit to certain stretches of road for particular periods of time or particular days. Outside these times or days, the usual speed limit at that location is in force.

An example of a periodic speed limit is one used near school grounds. One way to show this special limit is through a standard upright sign with an information plate underneath that shows the periods and days when the speed limit applies.

Electronic periodic
speed sign

Electronic periodic
speed sign at
school

Another way of showing the speed limit is an electronic speed limit sign which when lit up shows the speed limit in white numbers within a red border against a black background. Outside the special speed limit periods, the sign remains blank. Sometimes the electronic sign can be mounted on a grey backing board with two amber lights, which may flash when the sign is lit up.

The sign School Children Crossing Ahead that includes two amber flashing lamps may appear beside periodic speed limit signs to alert you to the presence of school children.

You **must not** break the periodic speed limits while they are in force.

Checking speed

From time to time and on various stretches of road, Gardaí may use certain equipment to check if vehicles are obeying the speed limit. It is against the law to supply, carry or use any device that can detect or interfere with any speed monitoring equipment under Garda control.

Speed camera ahead

Speed limits for vehicles

Some drivers **must** obey speed limits for their vehicles as well as speed limits for the roads on which they are travelling.

The table below outlines the speed limits that apply to different vehicles.

Vehicle speed limit	Type of vehicle to which it applies	
65 kilometres an hour (65km/h) On all roads	A single or double deck bus or coach designed for carrying standing passengers	
80 kilometres an hour (80km/h) On all roads except motorways	A goods vehicle with a maximum authorised mass (MAM) of more than 3,500 kilograms	
90 kilometres an hour (90km/h) On motorways	A goods vehicle with a maximum authorised mass (MAM) of more than 3,500 kilograms	
80 kilometres an hour (80km/h) On all roads	Any vehicle towing a trailer, caravan, horsebox or other attachment	
80 kilometres an hour (80km/h) On all roads except motorways or dual carriageways	A single or double deck bus or coach that is not designed for carrying standing passengers	
100 kilometres an hour (100km/h) On motorways or dual carriageways where no lower speed limit is in place	A single or double deck bus or coach that is not designed for carrying standing passengers	

If the vehicle and road speeds are different, the driver **must** obey the lower of the two. For example, if a bus designed to carry standing passengers is travelling on a road with a speed limit of 80km/h, it cannot travel faster than its vehicle speed limit of 65km/h. But if it is travelling on a road with a speed limit of 50km/h, it **must** obey this limit regardless of the maximum speed at which it might otherwise be allowed to travel.

Stopping distance for cars

Many drivers have a false belief that if the car in front starts braking, they can react, brake and come to a stop, still leaving the same distance between the two vehicles.

The total minimum stopping distance of your vehicle depends on four things:

- ◯ your perception time,
- ◯ your reaction time,
- ◯ your vehicle reaction time, and
- ◯ your vehicle braking capability.

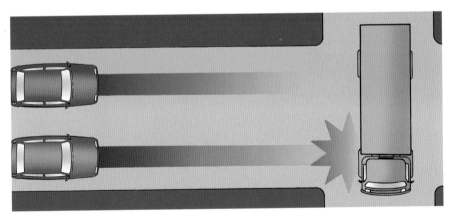

Your perception time is how long it takes you to see a hazard and for your brain to realise it is a hazard requiring you to take immediate action. This can be as long as 0.25 to 0.5 of a second or more.

Your reaction time is how long you take to move your foot from the accelerator to the brake pedal once your brain understands you are in danger. Your reaction time can vary from 0.25 to 0.75 of a second or more. It can be as long as 1.5 seconds.

These first two components of stopping distance are down to you, and they can be affected by alcohol, drugs, tiredness, fatigue or lack of concentration. A perception and reaction time of 4 seconds at 100km/h means the car travels 110 metres before the brakes are applied (this is more than the length of a football pitch).

Once you apply the brake pedal it will take time for your vehicle to react. This depends on the condition of your vehicle and, in particular, the condition of the braking system.

The final factor that determines your total minimum stopping distance is the vehicle's braking capability. This depends on many things, for example:

- brakes;
- tyre pressure, tread and grip;
- the weight of the vehicle;
- the vehicle's suspension; and
- road surface.

Table 5: The RSA recommend you allow a minimum stopping distance under dry conditions of (see table below):

Speed (km/h)	Minimum Reaction Distance (m)	Minimum Braking Distance (m)	Total Minimum Stopping Distance (m)
30 km/h	6	6	12
40 km/h	8	10	18
50 km/h	10	15	25
60 km/h	12	21	33

Speed (km/h)	Minimum Reaction Distance (m)	Minimum Braking Distance (m)	Total Minimum Stopping Distance (m)
80 km/h	16	36	52
100 km/h	20	50	70
120 km/h	24	78	102

Source Transport Research Laboratory, UK, 2012, © Road Safety Authority, 2012

Table 6: The RSA recommend you allow a minimum stopping distance under wet conditions of (see table below):

Speed (km/h)	Minimum Reaction Distance (m)	Minimum Braking Distance (m)	Total Minimum Stopping Distance (m)
20 km/h	4	5	9
30 km/h	6	10	16
40 km/h	8	17	25
50 km/h	10	26	36
60 km/h	12	37	49
70 km/h	14	50	64
80 km/h	16	65	81
100 km/h	20	101	121
120 km/h	24	145	169

Source Transport Research Laboratory, UK, 2012, © Road Safety Authority, 2012

It is worth noting that from 50km/h to 100km/h, the total braking distance of your car can increase from at least 26 metres to at least 101 metres. When you double the speed of your car, you multiply the total braking distance nearly four times.

Remember a 5km/h difference in your speed could be the difference between life and death for a vulnerable road user like a pedestrian.

- Hit by a car at 60km/h, 9 out of 10 pedestrians will be killed.
- Hit by a car at 50km/h, 5 out of 10 of pedestrians will be killed.
- Hit by a car at 30km/h, 1 out of 10 pedestrians will be killed.

Source RoSPA UK

The RSA recommend you allow a minimum overall stopping distance of (see table below):

Total Minimum Stopping Distance (m)

Source Transport Research Laboratory, UK, 2012, © Road Safety Authority, 2012

Skidding

Any factor which reduces the grip of your tyres on the road is a possible source of skidding. Wet or greasy roads, overloading, worn or improperly inflated tyres, mud, leaves, ice, snow, harsh acceleration, sudden braking, or excessive speed for the conditions can all cause or contribute to a skid.

'Aquaplaning' occurs when a car is being driven on a wet road and a film of water builds up between the tyres and the road surface.

When that happens, the car loses contact with the road, and braking and steering are affected.

REMEMBER

Distances outlined above are to be treated as absolute minimums: the average stopping distance can be significantly longer.

Section 9:

Junctions and roundabouts

//

This section outlines the correct way to approach and drive at junctions and roundabouts.

Junctions

If you see a 'Stop' sign (shown below), you **must** stop at the sign or at the stop line on the road, if provided, even if there is no traffic on the road you would like to enter.

Stop

If you see a 'Yield' sign or yield line (shown below), you **must** slow down, but you do not have to stop completely unless you need to wait for any oncoming traffic to pass.

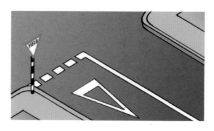

Géill Slí

Section 6 has more information on these and other regulatory signs.

Right of way

- Traffic travelling straight ahead in either direction along a major road generally has right of way at all times.

- If you are at a junction where the roads are of equal importance, the traffic on your right has right of way. You must let that traffic pass before you move on. It is important to understand that the right of way is not an absolute right. You must proceed with caution while showing regard for other users of the road.

- If you are approaching a T junction, the traffic already on the road you are joining has right of way. This means any traffic on the road ending at the junction must wait for the other traffic to pass before turning left or right.

- If you are turning right at a junction, the traffic coming straight through the junction from the opposite direction has right of way.

- If you plan to turn right at a junction and a vehicle from the opposite direction wants to turn into the same road, the vehicle that is turning left has right of way. If yours is the vehicle turning right, you must wait for the other vehicle to turn first.

- If you are approaching a junction with a major road, you must yield to other traffic. This means giving right of way or letting them pass before you enter the road you are joining.

Vehicles do not have an automatic right of way on the road. The overriding rule is, in all circumstances, to proceed with caution.

You must always yield to:
- pedestrians already crossing at a junction;
- pedestrians on a zebra crossing;
- pedestrians on a pelican crossing when the amber light is flashing; and
- pedestrians and traffic when you are moving off from a stationary position (for example from your position at a stop sign or a parking space).

To avoid doubt and in the interest of road safety, a vehicle **should** always yield to pedestrians.

You **must** also yield to:

- traffic already turning at a junction;

- traffic in another lane when you wish to change lanes; and

- traffic on a public road when you are coming out of a private entrance.

Stop, look, listen, and look again. This is your duty when entering the roadway.

Motorists **should** watch for cyclists emerging from the end of a cycle track, and watch for mopeds and motorcycles emerging from junctions. Bicycles, mopeds and motorcycles might be difficult to see because of their small size.

It is important to understand that the right of way is not an absolute right of way. You **must** proceed with caution, having regard for other road users.

Turning right from a major road onto a minor road

- Check your mirrors and blind spots well in advance for traffic following behind you and give a right turn signal.

- As soon as you can do so safely, take up a position just left of the middle of the road or in the space provided for right-turning traffic.

- Where possible, leave room for other vehicles to pass on the left.

- Do not turn the steering wheel until you are ready to make the turn.

- When a safe gap occurs in oncoming traffic, finish your turn so that you enter the left-hand side of the road into which you are turning.

- Do not cut the corner when you turn. Do not make a 'swan neck' by passing the correct turning point and then having to turn back into the road you want to enter.

Turning right from a minor road onto a major road

- Check your mirrors well in advance for traffic following behind you and give a right turn signal.

- As soon as you can do so safely, take up a position just left of the middle of the road.

- If you are at a junction controlled by a Stop or a Yield sign, wait at the entrance to the junction until the road is clear in both directions.

- Where possible, leave room for other vehicles to pass on the left.

- When a safe gap occurs in traffic coming from both directions, finish your turn so that you enter the left-hand side of the road onto which you are turning.

- Be alert for road markings which direct you to follow a certain course.

Turning right at a crossroads

When turning right at a crossroads and a car coming from the opposite direction is also turning right, if possible you should both try to turn back to back (pictured below). This allows you and the other driver to see oncoming traffic and allows the traffic to see you.

Turning back to back

If you cannot do this, you may turn near-side to near-side if necessary. This means starting the turn while the vehicles are still facing each other.

Turning near side to near side

Turning right from a one-way street

Drive as close as you safely can to the right-hand side of the one-way street. Look out for areas where two lanes may be allowed for turning right.

Turning left from a major road to a minor road

- Check your mirrors well in advance for traffic following behind you.

- Give a left-turn signal and, when safe, slow down.

- Keep as close as you safely can to the left-hand edge of the road, using your mirrors to watch for cyclists or motorcyclists coming up on your left.

- Watch for flashing amber arrows that allow you to proceed to the left if no traffic is approaching from the right.

- Where possible, leave room for other vehicles to pass on the right.

- Make the turn, keeping close to the left-hand edge. Do not hit or mount the kerb.

Turning left from a minor road to a major road

- Check your mirrors well in advance for traffic following behind you.

- Give a left turn signal and slow down.

- If you are at a junction controlled by a Stop or a Yield sign, wait at the entrance to the junction until the road is clear.

- Watch for flashing amber arrows that allow you to proceed to the left if no traffic is approaching from the right.

- If a left-turn slip lane is provided, you **should** use it.

- When it is safe, finish your turn so that you enter the left-hand side of the road onto which you are turning.

Take care not to swing wide when you turn and always give way to pedestrians and cyclists crossing the junction before you start any turn.

Yellow box junctions

These junctions consist of patterns of criss-cross yellow lines.

> **REMEMBER**
>
> **You must not enter the yellow box junction unless you can clear it without stopping.**

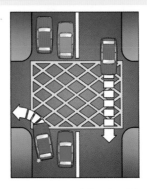

An exception is when you want to turn right. In this case, you may enter the yellow box junction while waiting for a gap in traffic coming from the opposite direction. However, don't enter the box if to do so would block other traffic that has the right of way.

Do 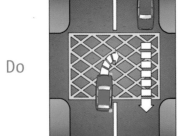 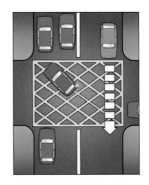 Don't

Yellow box junctions can also be found at railway level crossings or tramway crossings. Never enter these yellow box junctions unless you can leave them without stopping. Section 6 has more information on traffic signs and road markings.

Junctions and dual carriageways

Dual carriageways are roads with two or more lanes of traffic travelling in each direction. The outer or right-hand lane in each direction is the lane nearest to the centre of the dual carriageway.

You **must** normally drive in the left-hand lane of a dual carriageway. You may use the outer lane of a two-lane or three-lane dual carriageway only:

- for overtaking; and

- when intending to turn right a short distance ahead.

Turning left onto a dual carriageway

- Drive as close as you safely can to the left-hand edge of the approach road.

- Watch for oncoming traffic.

- Take the turn when it is safe to do so.

- Keep to the left-hand lane on the dual carriageway and build up your speed to that of the normal flow of traffic, subject to the speed limits and road conditions.

Crossing a dual carriageway or joining it by turning right

- When it is safe to do so, wait in the median space (the space in the central dividing strip) until there is a safe gap in traffic.

- Finish your crossing or turn into the second half of the dual carriageway and build up your speed to that of the normal flow of traffic, subject to speed limits and prevailing road conditions.

If another vehicle is already blocking the median space, wait on the minor road until there is enough space to clear the first half of the road without stopping on the carriageway. If the median is too narrow for your vehicle, wait on the minor road until you can clear both sides of the carriageway, and complete your turn in one go.

When driving a large vehicle, it is generally not safe to treat each half of the dual carriageway as a separate road. You **should** remain on the minor road until you can cross both sides of the dual carriageway without having to stop.

Always take care when you are behind large vehicles or vehicles towing trailers when they are turning. Remember, a long vehicle or combination needs extra room to finish a turn. Cyclists, motorcyclists and pedestrians, in particular, **should** be extra careful when near these vehicles.

Turning right from a dual carriageway

- Follow the normal procedure (see below) and move into the right-hand lane. If there is a deceleration lane, move into it.

- At the junction, turn into the median space and wait for a safe gap in traffic.

- When it is safe to do so, finish your turn and move into the left-hand lane of the road you are entering.

Roundabouts

Not every roundabout is the same. They are different shapes and sizes and can have different numbers of exits. Some are controlled by traffic lights.

The purpose of a roundabout is:

- to reduce delays – traffic flows smoothly compared to the stop and go traffic at normal intersections such as at traffic lights.

- to significantly reduce the risk of collisions.

- to reduce pollution – emissions from vehicles on roundabouts are less than they would be at traffic light junctions.

Golden Rule

This 'golden rule' should help motorists to drive safely at any roundabout regardless of the number of exits:

Think of the roundabout as a clock.

- If taking any exit from the 6 o'clock to the 12 o'clock position, motorists should generally approach in the left-hand lane.

- If taking any exit between the 12 o'clock to the 6 o'clock positions, motorists should generally approach in the right-hand lane.

- If there are road markings showing you what lane you should be in, follow those directions. Traffic conditions might sometimes mean you have to take a different approach but, in the main, the 'golden rule' will help you to drive safely on almost any roundabout.

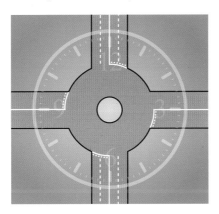

Approaching a roundabout

○ Conditions at roundabouts may vary. When you are coming up to a roundabout, look for directional arrows, road markings or signs which might be indicating which lane you should use for the exit you're taking.

○ Move into the correct lane in good time. Use the 12 o'clock 'golden rule' to help you plan a safe course of action unless road signs indicate otherwise.

○ Treat the roundabout as a junction. You **must** yield to traffic coming from the right, but keep moving if the way is clear.

Making a left turn

Approach in the left-hand lane, indicate 'left' as you approach, and continue until you have taken the left exit.

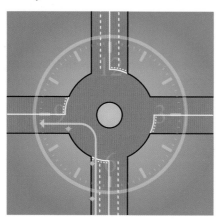 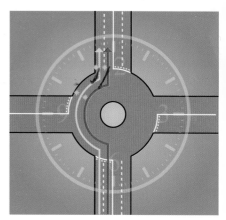

Going straight ahead (or any exit to the left of 12 o'clock)

Approach in the left-hand lane (unless road markings say otherwise) but do not indicate 'left' until you have passed the exit before the one you intend to take. Where traffic conditions dictate otherwise, for example a long line of traffic in the left lane signalling left or roadworks in the left lane, you may follow the course shown by the red line.

When leaving the roundabout take extra care at all exits, checking for other road users – for example, cyclists and motorcyclists who may be continuing on the roundabout.

Taking any later exits (those past 12 o'clock – right)

Approach in the right-hand lane (unless road markings say otherwise), indicate 'right' on your approach and leave your indicator on until you have passed the exit before the one you intend to take. Then change to the 'left' turn indicator. Move over towards the left on the roundabout and continue signalling left to leave.

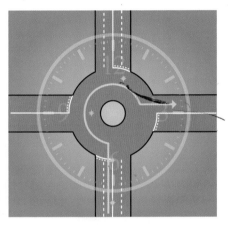 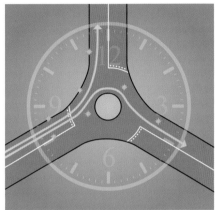

In all cases watch out for and give plenty of room to:

- o pedestrians who may be crossing the approach and exit roads,

- o traffic crossing in front of you on the roundabout, especially vehicles intending to leave by the next exit,

- o traffic that may be straddling lanes or positioned incorrectly,

- o motorcyclists,

- o cyclists and horse riders who may stay in the left-hand lane and signal right if they intend to continue round the roundabout,

- o long vehicles (including those towing trailers), which might have to take a different course approaching or on the roundabout because of their length. Watch out for their signals.

REMEMBER

Conditions at roundabouts may vary. Exercise caution at all times. In particular, be aware of traffic signs, traffic lights, road markings and traffic coming from your right when approaching roundabouts.

Section 10:

Parking

///

This section covers the rules on parking safely.

Parking

General rules

- Where possible, park in the direction of traffic flow.

- Park close to, and parallel with, the kerb or edge of the road, except at any location where straight or angled parking bays are marked out on the surface of the road.

- Where a parking bay is marked out on a road, you **must** park your vehicle fully within the parking space.

- Apply the handbrake.

- Switch off the engine.

- Leave the vehicle in first gear or reverse, or, in the case of an automatic, select P.

- Before opening any doors, check for other road users nearby, in particular motorcyclists, cyclists and pedestrians.

- Open your doors only when you need to and keep them open only for as long as necessary.

- Get out of your vehicle only when it is safe and you and your passengers are not blocking other road users.

- Passengers **should** exit on the kerbside.

- Lock your vehicle as you leave it.

- You **should not** leave headlights on when parked.

How to make sure your vehicle is parked safely

Make sure you do not interfere with normal traffic flow and that your vehicle does not disturb, block or endanger other road users.

Dos ✓	Don'ts ✗
Do park as close as possible to the kerb or edge of the road.	**Don't** park opposite another vehicle on a narrow road.
Do make sure the sides of your vehicle are parallel to the kerb or edge, unless a traffic sign indicates otherwise.	**Don't** double park.
Do park facing in the same direction as the traffic.	**Don't** park at roadworks.
Do make sure your vehicle can be seen at night.	**Don't** park at the entrance or exit of a fire station, Garda station, ambulance station or hospital.
Do park courteously, without blocking other road users' views of a traffic signal or the road ahead.	**Don't** park where you would block other road users' views of a traffic signal or the road ahead.
Do park where you would not block the entrance to a property unless you have the owner's permission.	**Don't** park where parking is forbidden by traffic signs or road markings (see section 6).
	Don't leave headlights switched on when parking at the side of the road, or just off the side of the road.

REMEMBER

Drivers can quickly become dazzled and disorientated by headlights of parked or stopped vehicles. If you need to have lights on in these circumstances, you should use only 'side' or 'parking' lights. You should not leave headlights on when parked.

The following traffic signs and road markings show where parking is **not** allowed or is allowed **only at certain times.**

Traffic signs

These signs and their information plates show that you can park only during certain periods (sign 1) or outside certain periods (sign 2).

Sign 1	*Sign 2*
Parking permitted	*Parking prohibited*

The sign below shows a clearway – an area of road that **must** be kept clear for moving traffic during certain times of the day (usually busy periods). The times when stopping or parking is prohibited are shown on an information plate under the sign.

Other vehicles may stop during these times only if they are waiting in a line of traffic, but they are not allowed to park, even if disc or metered parking is normally available.

Clearway

Road markings

This single yellow line usually has an upright information plate nearby.
Together, the road marking and information plate mean you **must not** park
during the times shown.

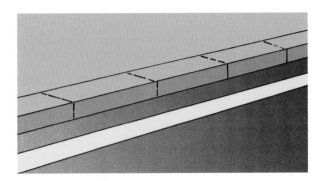

The double yellow lines mean no parking at any time.

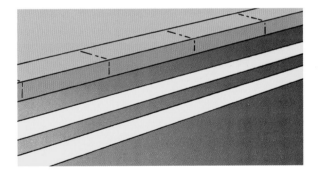

No parking

Even if you do not see a particular 'no parking' sign or yellow line on the road, you **must not** stop or park:

- in a designated disabled persons parking space unless you display a 'reserved for a person with a disability' permit. Wheelchair users need to use the extra-wide, special parking bay to open their car door fully. This will allow a person to get from a wheelchair to a vehicle or from a vehicle to a wheelchair. Normal parking bays are too narrow to give the access required by wheelchair users, so other road users **must not** park in the designated disabled persons parking spaces. It is an offence to do so.

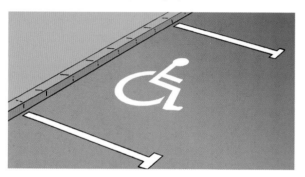

- where there are white or yellow zig-zag lines on either side of pedestrian lights or either side of pelican or zebra crossings;

- wholly or partly on a zebra or pelican crossing or at pedestrian lights;

- 15 metres before or 5 metres after a pedestrian crossing or traffic lights;

- near a school entrance where there are yellow zig-zag lines along the edge of the roadway enclosing the words 'SCHOOL KEEP CLEAR';

- near an entrance or exit from a Fire, Ambulance or Garda station;

- within an area marked as a bus stop or taxi rank - white roadway markings line the areas and, in addition show the word 'BUS' at a bus stop and 'TAXIS' at a taxi rank;

- where there is a single or double continuous white line along the centre of the road;

- wholly or partly on a footpath, a grass margin, a cycle lane or track or a median strip;

- within 5 metres of a road junction unless parking spaces are clearly marked;

- on a part of a road reserved for casual trading during trading hours;

- in a contra-flow bus lane at any time or in a with-flow bus lane during the hours the bus lane is in force;

- in a loading bay (reserved for goods vehicles to use while loading or unloading goods for a maximum period of 30 minutes) – roadway markings show the word 'LOADING' repeated across the entrance of the parking area;

- in an entrance or exit for vehicles to or from a premises, unless authorised by the occupier of the premises;

- in a tram lane during the period the tram lane is in force (tram lanes operate on a 24-hour basis unless an alternative period is shown on an information plate beside the lane);

- on the approach to a level crossing;

- where the kerb has been lowered to help wheelchair users.

REMEMBER

You must not park in any way which interferes with the normal flow of traffic, or which obstructs or endangers other road users.

You must never park:

- at a corner, a bend, the brow of a hill or on a hump-back bridge;

- where there is a sharp dip in the road; or

- anywhere that blocks the view of a school warden or junior school warden service – this restriction does not apply to a vehicle displaying a disabled persons parking permit.

Disc parking

Disc parking operates in built-up areas to restrict parking during certain times of the day. You will see the regulatory sign and information plate pictured below in areas covered by disc parking. When you park, you **must** buy a disc for a set period of time and leave the parking space by the time this period ends. You **must not** park again in the same street within one hour of leaving a disc-parking space. The restriction does not apply to a vehicle displaying a parking permit for a person with a disability.

Luain - Ooine
0700 - 0930
MON. - FRI.

Diosca-Pháirceail
1 uair
DISC PARKING
1 hour
Luan - Sath.
08.30
TO
18.30
MON.- SAT.

Parking permitted   Disc parking

Clamping or removing vehicles

Some local authorities have introduced systems to combat illegal parking. If your vehicle is parked illegally, a clamp may be fixed to a wheel, or your vehicle may be towed to another place and have a clamp attached there, or your vehicle could be removed and locked up in a vehicle pound. You **must** then pay a fee to remove the clamp or have your vehicle returned to you.

Dangerous parking

If you park in a way that is likely to cause danger to other road users, for example, if it forces a pedestrian out onto the roadway, a Garda can decide that you have committed an offence of dangerous parking, for which you may be liable to a fixed charge of €80 and/or up to 5 penalty points.

REMEMBER

Always ensure not to endanger other road users – particularly vulnerable road users – when parking. In particular, never park on a footpath.

Section 11:
Motorways and tunnels

///

Motorways are roads that help reduce journey times by separating traffic and removing road junctions. They are probably the safest way of moving large volumes of traffic, mainly because they remove the risk of head-on collision. However, compared with other types of road, they carry a greater risk of pile-ups.

This section covers the rules on who can drive on a motorway, the meaning of motorway signs, how to overtake safely and how to join and leave a motorway safely.

See section 25 for a list of common signs you will see on a motorway.

Motorway signs		What they mean
Motorway ahead NO L drivers Vehicles under 50cc. Slow vehicles (under 50 km/h). Invalid - carriages. Pedal - cycles. Pedestrians. Animals	**Motorway ahead**	There is an entrance to a motorway ahead and the road users listed on the sign must not enter the motorway.
M7	**Entry to motorway**	The road user is now entering a motorway and must obey motorway rules. This sign usually appears beside the 'Motorway ahead' sign.
≡	**Countdown sign**	The driver is 300 metres from the next exit off the motorway.
≡	**Countdown sign**	The driver is 200 metres from the next exit.
╱	**Countdown sign**	The driver is 100 metres from the next exit.

Motorway signs		What they mean
Motorway ends 500m ahead		There are 500 metres to the end of the motorway.
End of motorway		The driver has reached the end of the motorway.
Lane gain sign		An additional lane is joining the motorway.
Next exit sign		Indicates distance to the next exit and supplementary routes.

General rules

The signs below appear as you are about to enter or join a motorway. The sign on the left shows that the following **must not** enter a motorway:

Motorway ahead   Motorway ahead   Entry to motorway

- ○ people who do not hold a full driving licence for the category of vehicle they drive;

- ○ vehicles incapable of a speed of at least 50km/h;

- ○ vehicles with an engine capacity of 50cc. or less;

- ○ invalid carriages or motorised wheelchairs;

- ○ vehicles that do not use inflated tyres;

- ○ cyclists;

- ○ pedestrians; and

- ○ animals.

Motorway speed limits

The maximum speed limit on a motorway is 120km per hour unless:

- there are signs stating another speed limit – for example, warning signs to highlight roadworks – or

- you are driving a vehicle that is subject to a lower limit such as a bus or truck.

Remember, your total stopping distance at 120km per hour in dry conditions is 102 metres (27 car lengths). This is about the length of a soccer pitch.

- The ordinary speed limit for HGVs is 90km/h on motorways (where no lower speed limit is in place).

- The ordinary speed limit for buses (that are not designed for carrying standing passengers) is 100km/h on motorways or dual carriageways (where no lower speed limit is in place).

Joining the motorway

When entering the motorway, be careful and pay attention, and let traffic already on the motorway pass. You **must** follow the steps below when joining a motorway.

- Use the acceleration lane to build up your speed before merging into traffic on the motorway.

- Signal early to other motorists that you intend to merge.

- As you approach on the slip road, check in your mirrors and your blind spot for a safe gap in traffic in the left-hand lane of the motorway.

- Obey road signs and road markings.

- Do not drive on hatched markings before merging into traffic on the motorway.

- Give way to traffic already on the motorway.

- Adjust your speed as you join the motorway so you match, as near as possible, the general speed of traffic in that lane.

- Treat each lane change as a separate manoeuvre. Stay in the left-hand lane long enough to adjust to the speed of traffic before attempting to overtake.

On the motorway

- You must only drive ahead. No turning or reversing is permitted.

- You must progress at a speed and in a way that avoids interference with other motorway traffic.

- You must not drive on any part of the motorway that is not a carriageway – for example, a hard shoulder – except in case of emergency.

- You must not stop or park on any part of the motorway unless your vehicle breaks down or you are signalled by a Garda to do so.

- You must not pick up or set down anybody on a motorway.

> ### REMEMBER
>
> **If you find yourself driving against the flow of traffic, pull in immediately to the hard shoulder and stop. Contact the Gardaí by dialling 999 or 112. Do not attempt to turn your vehicle. Wait for help in a safe place.**

Using lanes properly

It is very important that you understand the purpose of each lane on a motorway. To help explain how and when to move from one lane to another, each lane is given a number. The picture below shows that Lane 1 is the lane nearest the hard shoulder. This is also known as the 'inside lane'. On a two-lane motorway, the lane nearest the central median is Lane 2 (also called the 'outside lane'). On a three-lane motorway, this lane is Lane 3.

Lane 1

The normal 'keep left' rule applies. Stay in this lane unless you are overtaking.

Lane 2

On a two-lane motorway, use this for overtaking only and move back into Lane 1 when you have finished. You may also use this lane to accommodate traffic merging from the left.

On a three-lane motorway, you may stay in this centre lane while there is slower moving traffic in Lane 1.

Lane 3

If you are travelling on a three-lane motorway, you **must** use this lane only if traffic in lanes 1 and 2 is moving in queues and you need to overtake or accommodate merging traffic. Once you've finished overtaking, move back to your left and allow faster traffic coming from behind to pass by.

You **must not** use the lane nearest the central median, that is, the outside lane (Lane 2 or Lane 3, depending on the number of lanes), if you are driving:

- a goods vehicle with a maximum authorised mass of more than 3,500 kilograms, such as a lorry or heavy goods vehicle;

- a vehicle towing a trailer, horsebox or caravan; or

- a single or double deck bus/coach that is designed for carrying standing passengers.

It is a fixed-charge offence of up to €120 and/or 3 penalty points for a vehicle listed above to drive on the outside lane of a motorway (which may be Lane 2 or Lane 3, depending on the number of lanes).

You may use it, however, in exceptional circumstances when you cannot proceed in the inner lane because of an obstruction ahead.

A single or double-deck bus/coach that is not designed for carrying standing passengers may travel in the outside lane of a motorway and a driver of such a vehicle will not be guilty of an offence if they do so.

Keeping your distance

Section 8 covers the 'two second rule' to help you keep a safe distance behind the vehicle in front. Use this rule on motorways – driving too close reduces your ability to stop safely, and significantly reduces your vision ahead.

When in a queue, your instinct may be to get closer to the vehicle in front to protect your position. Please remember that you **must** leave enough room in front of you to allow you to stop safely.

Signalling

Once on a motorway, you **must** make a signal before every move. For example, moving from Lane 3 to Lane 1 involves two separate stages.

- ○ In stage one you signal once to move from Lane 3 to Lane 2.

- ○ In stage two you signal again to move from Lane 2 to Lane 1.

An indicator is not a right of way.

Before you start to manoeuvre, you must exercise due care and attention with particular heed to other users of the road, prevailing road conditions and how your driving will impact other road users.

Checking traffic around you

Check your mirrors regularly, as you need to have a constant picture in your mind of what's going on all around you. Be very aware of your blind spots as well.

As a driver, you **must** be able to stop within a distance that you can see to be clear and you **must** drive having due regard to other users of the road. Therefore you **should** avoid staying in other drivers' blind spots. Keep your eyes moving – avoid looking only at the vehicle immediately ahead. Instead, scan up the queue. Use your view to drive smoothly and avoid unnecessary braking. If you notice traffic slowing down sharply, use your hazard warning lights to warn traffic behind you.

Before changing lane, remember 'mirror, signal, mirror, manoeuvre'. Remember that traffic may be coming from behind you at speed. Checking your mirrors at least twice helps you judge this approach speed and will help you to see vehicles travelling in your blind spots.

Avoid causing another driver to brake or change lane to accommodate you while you are on the motorway (aside from joining it). Learn to read the traffic around you. A vehicle in your mirror on the motorway with its right indicator flashing is trying to tell you that it's catching up on you and intends to overtake your vehicle.

Overtaking

Overtake only on the right, unless traffic is travelling in slow moving queues and the traffic queue on your right is travelling more slowly than you are. If you intend to move from a slower lane to a faster lane, adjust your speed first.

Before you start to overtake, remember 'mirror, signal, mirror, manoeuvre', and look in your blind spots. Check that the way is clear (behind and ahead) and signal well in advance.

Remember that traffic will be travelling a lot faster than on ordinary roads. Be particularly careful at dusk, during darkness, and in poor weather conditions when it is more difficult to judge speed, distance and stopping distance. Signal and return to your original lane as soon as possible.

Gantries

Gantries are structures used to display traffic signs above traffic lanes on motorways and dual-carriageways. They are common and display important information, so make sure you pay attention to them as well as to other signs along the side of the road.

Variable message signs

Variable message signs such as the one displayed below are used on motorways to provide messages and information to motorists and to warn of incidents that may affect traffic conditions and journey times.

Motorists **should** pay attention to these signs at all times.

Typical LED VMS

Leaving the motorway

The signs below show the distance to the next exit on a motorway. Plan well ahead and use these signs to position yourself in good time so you can get into lane early.

| 2km to next exit | 300m to next exit | 200m to next exit | 100m to next exit |

When you leave the motorway, you will first enter a deceleration lane. If possible, keep up your speed until you enter this lane, but then slow down and check for signs showing a lower speed limit. Use your speedometer to make sure you are obeying the reduced limit. Remember that the slip roads and link roads between motorways may include sharp bends.

If you miss your exit, drive on to the next exit. You **must not** attempt to cross the ghost island or reverse back up the hard shoulder.

When you leave a motorway, or it comes to an end, you will see the signs below.

Motorway ends
1km ahead

Motorway ends
500m ahead

End of motorway

Rest areas, lay-bys and motorway services

The best advice is to plan your journey to avoid having to stop on motorways if at all possible. However, it is important to take regular breaks to rest at appropriate intervals when travelling long distances. Before you start your journey, you should plan where you will stop to rest and use motorway services. The map below shows rest and service areas. Areas marked P are lay-bys where you can stop safely if necessary. They have no facilities. Do not walk on or close to the hard shoulder or motorway lanes. Take care when re-joining the motorway (see advice on page 141).

As the above map shows, there are various motorway services available throughout the country. Development of these motorway services is ongoing. Further information as to the available motorway services can be found on the National Roads Authority website, *www.nra.ie.*

The following signs indicate the motorway services which may be available:

Fuel	Garage and repairs	Telephone	Public toilets

| Restaurant | Refreshments | Picnic area | Accommodation | Information point |

Stopping and parking

You may only stop or park on the motorway when:

- your car breaks down,

- a Garda signals you to do so,

- there is an emergency (such as a crash),

- there are roadworks, or

- you are at a toll plaza.

Before you begin a long motorway journey, make sure your vehicle:

- is fit to carry out a long journey at motorway speeds,

- has the correct tyre pressure,

- has enough oil and coolant, and

- has enough fuel to at least take you to the next petrol station.

Also make sure that any loads carried or towed are secure and that you have enough money or a suitable pass if you are using a tolled motorway.

What to do if your vehicle breaks down

- Look out for marked parking areas.

- Move your vehicle to the hard shoulder. Park as near to the left as you can. If you cannot do this, take steps to warn other drivers such as switching on your hazard warning lights.

- Use the roadside phone to contact the Gardaí. This automatically lets them know your exact location. If you cannot use this phone, use your mobile but be aware they will need information about your location.

- Do not place any warning device such as a triangle on the motorway as it is too dangerous.

- Never try to do repairs yourself on the hard shoulder.

- Wear a high visibility vest. Always carry at least two in the vehicle.

- Do not walk on the motorway. Leave your vehicle through the left-hand door and make sure your passengers do the same. Leave animals in the vehicle or, in an emergency, keep them under control on the verge.

- Make sure that passengers keep away from the motorway lanes and hard shoulder, and keep children under control.

○ Wait for help on the embankment side of the motorway well behind the crash barrier.

○ If, for some reason, you are unable to follow the above advice, you should stay in your vehicle with your safety belt securely fastened and switch on your hazard lights.

○ Before you re-join the motorway after a breakdown, build up your speed on the hard shoulder before merging into traffic. Be aware that other vehicles may have stopped on the hard shoulder.

○ Many motorways (and dual carriageways) now include important information about location and direction of travel on the surface of the hard shoulder. This information includes Location Reference Indicator (LRI) signs and Location Reference Marking (LRM) signs and is aimed at assisting road users in accurately communicating their location in the event of an incident or breakdown.

An LRI sign is an upright sign on a pole and will include the following information:

○ the motorway/ dual carriageway road number you are travelling on;

○ the direction of travel – this can only be one of N, S, E and W; and

○ the distance in kilometres from the start point of the motorway/ dual carriageway.

Example of motorway LRI sign   *Example of dual carriageway LRI sign*

LRM signs are painted in the hard shoulder parallel to the road and supplement the LRI upright signs. The LRM indicates:

- the route and the direction of travel (the example below indicates that it Is the M7, heading west);

- the distance from the start of the route (the example below indicates a distance of 72.5km from the start of the M7, heading west)

- the direction to the nearest emergency telephone.

Example of LRM sign

Obstructions

If you become aware of something blocking the flow of traffic ahead, use the roadside telephone or a mobile phone to tell the Gardaí. Do not attempt to remove it yourself. Do not use a mobile phone whilst driving.

Driving in fog

Dense fog seriously reduces your visibility and makes driving very dangerous. Our advice is to switch on dipped headlights and fog lamps, reduce your speed and keep a safe distance from the vehicle in front. If the fog closes in, reduce your speed further and take your time getting to your destination.

The added danger posed by dense fog is that a collision involving one vehicle can quickly involve many others, especially if driving too fast and too close to one another. The greatest risk is of a multiple-vehicle pile-up on roads with higher speeds such as motorways and dual carriageways. As you enter fog, check your mirrors and slow down. Use your foot brake lightly so that your lights warn following drivers.

Toll plazas

When approaching a toll, reduce your speed appropriately. Always leave a safe gap between your vehicle and the vehicle in front. All toll roads in Ireland, with the exception of the M50 eFlow barrier-free tolling system, are managed by a conventional barrier-operated toll plaza. For these toll roads, the toll payment options are:

- manual lanes with a toll booth attendant;

- automatic coin machine lanes; and
- payment by electronic toll tag.

Toll lane signage

This sign shows that a toll collector manually operates the lane and that all methods of payments are accepted.

This eToll sign is the sign for electronic toll collection. (This is available in all lanes.)

This sign shows that this is an automatic coin machine lane and that coins are the only method of payment accepted. No change will be given in this lane.

This sign shows that credit cards are accepted in this lane.

Heavy goods vehicles (HGVs) are not permitted in this lane.

Lane open.

Lane closed.

Tunnels

The general rules of the road and the Road Traffic Acts apply, but specific road safety issues apply when you are approaching, driving through or leaving a tunnel.

Approaching the tunnel

- Check you have enough fuel in your vehicle before entering the tunnel.

- Remove sunglasses.

- Switch on dipped headlights.

- If available, tune in to the designated FM radio station as this will let you hear safety instructions during your journey. The station frequency will be displayed on an information sign at the entrance to the tunnel.

- Keep a safe distance from the vehicle in front. Remember, you're entering a tunnel and tailgating could create an emergency. The recommended minimum safe distance for a car or motorcycle is 50 metres and for all other vehicles 100 metres. Always remember the 'two second rule'.

- Be aware there are restrictions on the use of tunnels by Heavy Goods Vehicles (HGVs).

  - The maximum permissible height will be signposted. You must check this before you enter the tunnel.

  - Wide loads may not be permitted. If you are carrying a wide load, you must contact the tunnel operators well in advance to see if the load is allowed.

  - Vehicle size – there may be a ban on the use of the right-hand lane in a tunnel by large goods vehicles or other non-passenger vehicles if the number of axles on the vehicle equals or is more than the figure shown on a regulatory sign provided on the approach road to a tunnel.

For detailed information contact the tunnel operator.

In the tunnel

- Keep in lane and do not overtake.

- You must not drive in the right-hand lane in a motorway tunnel if you are driving a type of vehicle prohibited from using this lane, that is a HGV of more than 3,500 kilograms, a vehicle towing a trailer, horsebox or caravan, or a single or double deck bus/coach that is designed for carrying standing passengers.

- Do not turn or reverse.

- Do not stop, except in case of emergency.

- Obey the speed limits. There are two forms of speed limit signs.

  - a standard speed limit sign applies where there is a fixed speed limit. You must obey the speed limit and remember this is the maximum permitted speed, not the required speed.

  - where the speed limit can vary, you will see variable message signs, which are black squares with red circles and numbers in white or yellow throughout the tunnel. The speed limit is shown by the numbers and will vary according to traffic conditions and road safety considerations. You must obey the speed limit and remember this is the maximum permitted speed, not the required speed. 'Always remember the two-second rule.'

- Keep your distance. The recommended minimum safe distance for a car or motorcycle is 50 metres and for all other vehicles 100 metres.

Stopping

If you are instructed to stop, you **should** stop and:

- keep a safe distance between your vehicle and the vehicle in front;

- switch on your hazard warning lights;

- switch off your engine;

- check your radio for instructions from the tunnel operator;

- check all electronic signs in the tunnel for information; and

- if necessary, leave the tunnel using the nearest available pedestrian exit.

Breakdown or a crash

If there is a breakdown or a crash in the tunnel, you **should**:

- switch off your engine;
- switch on your hazard warning lights;
- check your radio for instructions;
- go to an emergency station and use the emergency phone to tell the tunnel operator; and
- check all electronic signs in the tunnel for information.

Fire in your vehicle

If there is smoke or fire in your vehicle, you **should**:

- switch off your engine;
- leave your vehicle immediately;
- go to an emergency station and use the emergency phone to tell the tunnel operator; and
- leave the tunnel by the nearest available exit.

Fire in another vehicle

If there is smoke or fire in another vehicle, you **should**:

- drive out of the tunnel if the fire is behind you; or
- if the fire is ahead of you, turn off your engine, leave the vehicle immediately, and leave the tunnel by the nearest emergency exit.

Leaving the tunnel

- Keep a safe speed and position on the roadway.
- Follow the road signs.

Signage in tunnels

Be aware that, as with all emergencies, care needs to be taken to find the safest evacuation route. Take note of information provided on signage to determine what action you **should** take.

Emergency (Tunnel) Lay-by

Fire Extinguisher and Telephone

Fire Extinguisher, Telephone and Lay-by

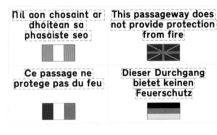

Emergency Station

Pedestrian Exit

Section 12:

Assisting Gardaí

///

An Garda Síochána are responsible for enforcing road traffic law. This section covers the Garda signals and instructions you **must** obey when on the road.

Signals

If a Garda is controlling traffic, their signals **override** all other signals from traffic lights. This means that if they signal you to stop, for example, you **must** do so even if a green light is showing. The signals and their meanings are shown below. You **must** understand them so you know how to respond when in traffic.

To beckon on traffic approaching from the front

To beckon on traffic approaching from either side

To halt traffic approaching from the front

To halt traffic approaching from behind

To halt traffic approaching from the front and behind

Instructions

You **must** do the following if a Garda asks you to:

- Show your driving licence, which you **must** carry at all times when driving.

- Allow the Garda to examine the insurance disc, tax disc, and, where relevant the NCT disc, all of which you **must** display on your vehicle.

- Produce a certificate of roadworthiness or NCT certificate, as appropriate, at a named Garda station within 10 days.

- Produce a valid motor insurance certificate to a Garda within 10 days of it being requested. A Garda may ask to see a valid motor insurance certificate any time up to a month after observing or reasonably believing that an uninsured vehicle has been used in a public place.

- Produce the vehicle registration certificate at any reasonable time.

- Stop your vehicle and allow a Garda to check it for defects.

- Give your name and address.

- Write out your signature.

- Give a sample of your breath. You may be required to provide a roadside breath sample if you have been involved in a crash, if you have committed a road traffic offence or if a Garda forms the opinion that you have consumed an intoxicant, such as alcohol or certain drugs.

- Perform 'impairment tests'. You may be required to perform impairment tests where a Garda suspects that you are driving under the influence of drugs. Before conducting such a test, a Garda will ascertain whether you have any disability or medical condition which you think might prevent you from participating in the relevant test.

A Garda may conclude from observing your ability to perform these tests that your ability to drive is impaired. It is an offence to refuse to perform impairment tests if required by a Garda.

Gardaí can set up Mandatory Alcohol Testing checkpoints (MATs) to take roadside breath samples without the need to form the opinion that you have consumed an intoxicant. It is a criminal offence to refuse to provide a sample.

If you are arrested for an offence related to alcohol and driving or refusing to give a roadside breath sample, you will be required to provide a sample of breath and blood or urine at a Garda station.

Gardaí may also require you to permit a nurse or doctor to take a blood or urine sample from you in situations where you have been involved in an accident in which you were driving and are attending at hospital. It is an offence to refuse to allow a doctor or nurse to take a sample in such situations (unless the doctor or nurse themselves refuse to take the sample on medical grounds).

Where a person is incapable of complying with this above requirement (for example, the driver is unconscious), the Gardaí may direct the doctor or nurse to take a sample of blood from the person. It is an offence for a person to refuse permission for that blood sample to be subsequently tested (unless they have a special or substantial reason for their refusal).

If a doctor advises the Garda that the taking of either a urine or blood sample from the person may adversely affect that person's health, the Garda will not make the above requirement of a person or give the above direction to a doctor/nurse.

Other controls on road users

- Officials from the Revenue Commissioners including Customs may also stop and examine vehicles.

- Your vehicle may also be impounded by a Revenue Official and/or Gardaí.

- You may also be stopped by the Gardaí working with Transport Officers from the Road Safety Authority who will check the tachograph and Operator's Licence.

What to do when an emergency service vehicle approaches

You need to know what to do when you see an emergency vehicle. You **must** react quickly, safely and carefully to allow emergency service vehicles to pass.

It is important to be alert and attentive at all times. You **should** keep noise levels in your vehicle at a level that allows you to hear the sirens from emergency vehicles.

Be alert at intersections and observe your surroundings as emergency service vehicles may come from behind you or from a secondary road.

You **should** also leave plenty of space between you and the vehicle in front when stopped in traffic. This will give you space to manoeuvre your vehicle if, for example, you need to pull in to let the emergency service vehicles pass – something you cannot do if you are sandwiched between two vehicles in traffic.

Gardaí, fire fighters and ambulances save lives in the course of their work and every second counts when they are responding to an emergency.

When an emergency vehicle approaches:

- Clear the way as soon as you can do so safely when you see the flashing lights and/or hear the sirens.

- Never mount the kerb unless you absolutely have to and, even then, only if you are certain that there are no pedestrians in the area.

- Check your rear mirror and both side mirrors to gauge the speed of the emergency vehicle and also look out for pedestrians, cyclists, motorcyclists and other road users. Indicate your intention to pull over. Pull over only in a place which has enough space for the emergency vehicle to pass you safely.

- Stay there until the emergency vehicle has passed. Watch out for other emergency vehicles as there may be more than one.

- Indicate that you are going to pull out again. When it is safe to do so, gradually merge back into traffic.

Never ever:

- Tailgate or overtake an emergency vehicle with lights or sirens unless directed to do so.

- Race after an emergency service vehicle to get through a traffic light.

- Break a red light or speed to allow emergency service vehicles to pass you unless you're directed to do so by the Gardaí or emergency service personnel.

- Brake suddenly or block the road.

- Overtake a moving emergency service vehicle that is displaying flashing lights.

Pedestrians, cyclists and motorcyclists

Pedestrians, cyclists and motorcyclists **should** look and listen for emergency service vehicles.

It is important to think about the route of the emergency service vehicle to make sure that you are not in its path. Keep in as far as possible on the correct side of the road.

If you are a pedestrian and there is an embankment or grass verge, you **should** use it (if it is safe to do so) in order to keep out of danger. If you are pushing a pram or buggy, this may not be possible so make sure that you keep in as far as possible. Try to anticipate the route that the emergency service vehicle is taking and attempt to alert the emergency service vehicle to your presence on the road.

If you have children with you, make sure that you are holding their hands at all times. It is important to wear hi-viz clothing at all times to make sure other road users can see you. Pedestrians **should** always wait until emergency service vehicles have passed before crossing the road at traffic lights, pedestrian lights, zebra crossings or pelican crossings.

For more information see 'Sharing the Road with Emergency Service Vehicles – some basic tips', available from *www.rsa.ie*.

Section 13:
Factors that affect safe driving

//

The main factors that can affect your driving are:

- alcohol;
- drugs (prescription and non-prescription);
- tiredness and fatigue;
- road rage or other forms of aggression.

Individually or together, these factors will:

- affect your judgment;
- slow your ability to react to and avoid hazards;
- cause you to lose concentration; and
- make you a less safe and socially responsible driver.

Alcohol

Alcohol is a major factor in crashes that lead to death and injury.

Research proves that even small amounts of alcohol affect your judgement and ability to drive.

> ### REMEMBER
>
> **The only safe advice is to NEVER EVER drink and drive. Could you live with the shame?**

There is no reliable way to tell how much you can drink before you exceed the legal limit. Our best advice is never ever drink and drive. Please check the current levels at *www.rsa.ie*.

The Gardaí may breathalyse any driver stopped at a mandatory alcohol checkpoint without the need to form any opinion in relation to the driver of the vehicle.

Gardaí **must** conduct mandatory testing of drivers for alcohol at the scene of a crash where someone has been injured, or of a driver who has been injured and removed to hospital.

In situations where a driver has been brought to hospital, the driver may be required by Gardaí to permit a nurse or doctor to take a blood or urine sample. It is an offence to refuse to allow a doctor or nurse to take a sample in such situations (unless the doctor or nurse themselves refuse to take the sample on medical grounds). Where the driver is incapable of complying with this above requirement (for example, the driver is unconscious), the Gardaí may direct the doctor or nurse to take a sample of blood from the person. It is an offence for a person to refuse permission for that blood sample to be subsequently tested (unless they have a special or substantial reason for their refusal).

If a doctor advises the Garda that the taking of either a urine or blood sample from the person may adversely affect that person's health, the Garda will not make the above requirement of a person or give the above direction to a doctor/nurse.

By law, drivers may be required to give a sample of breath in a Garda Station. Gardaí are allowed to make arrangements to take a blood or urine sample and have it analysed to check the level of alcohol. The result of these tests can be used as evidence when the driver's case goes to court.

Penalties for drink driving

Once stopped by An Garda Síochána, a driver may be tested for alcohol and taken to a Garda station for further testing. **In all cases**, if a driver fails a preliminary breath test at the roadside, they will be arrested and required to provide an evidential breath, blood or urine specimen at a Garda station.

The offence of refusing to provide a sample of blood, urine, or breath for evidential purposes will attract an automatic disqualification of four years for a first offence and six years for a second or subsequent offence.

Under the new system, if a driver is not already disqualified from holding a driving licence at the time of detection, or has not availed of the fixed penalty notice option in the preceding three years, and the BAC (Blood Alcohol Concentration) levels in the body do not exceed 100mg, they will be subsequently served with a fixed penalty notice. Court proceedings will not be initiated if payment of the fixed charge is made and the penalty accepted.

The penalties which apply are:

- If a driver is tested and their BAC is between 50mg and 80mg, they will be served an on-the-spot fixed penalty notice, receive a fine of €200 and 3 penalty points. The penalty points will remain on the licence record for three years.

- If a driver is tested and their BAC is between 80mg and 100mg, they will be served an on-the-spot fixed penalty notice, receive a fine of €400 and will be disqualified from holding a licence for six months.

- If a driver who is a learner, novice or professional driver is tested, and they are above the 20mg limit (but less than 80mg), they will be served with an on-the-spot fixed penalty notice, receive a fine of €200 and the person will be disqualified from holding a driving licence for three months.

Where a driver is tested and their BAC is above 100mg (or 80mg for a learner, novice or professional driver), or they have failed to pay a fixed penalty notice, they will have to go to court where the disqualification periods range from 1 to 6 years depending on the level of alcohol detected, and whether it is a first or subsequent offence.

> REMEMBER
>
> **Never ever drink and drive**

Drugs

It is against the law to drive a car, motor bike, truck, bus, pedal bike or an animal-drawn vehicle while 'under the influence of an intoxicant to such an extent as to be incapable of having control of the vehicle'.

Intoxicants include alcohol and drugs, whether taken separately or together. The word 'drugs' here includes legal prescribed and over the counter (OTC) medicines.

If a Garda suspects you of driving under the influence of drugs, they may require you to perform 'impairment tests'. Before conducting such tests, a Garda will ascertain whether you have any disability or medical condition which you think might prevent you from participating in the relevant test. These impairment tests may involve the performance of the following five tests:

- a 'pupil dilation' test;

- a test of your ability to balance;

- a 'walk and turn' test;

- a 'one leg stand' test; and

- a 'finger to nose' test.

It is an offence to refuse to perform impairment tests if required by a Garda.

A Garda may conclude from observing your ability to perform these tests that your ability to drive is impaired and consequently arrest you. The results of these tests may be used as evidence, along with any blood or urine samples taken and tested for the presence of any drugs, in order to convict you of driving while under the influence of an intoxicant.

Driver tiredness and fatigue

You **should not** drive while tired or fatigued. Research has shown that tired drivers are a major road safety risk, both to themselves and to others.

If you are tired and fighting sleep, you are likely to experience 'micro sleeps'. These episodes can last up to 10 seconds and can be experienced even when your eyes are open.

During a micro-sleep of even 4 seconds, your car can travel 100 metres (more than the length of a football pitch) without you being in control of your vehicle.

All drivers are at risk from driver tiredness but the following drivers are particularly high risk:

- Night workers

- People driving home after a night shift

- Lorry drivers

- Company car drivers

- Men (particularly those aged 18 – 24 and 50+)

- Skilled manual workers

Truck drivers fall into several of the above high-risk groups and need to be particularly careful.

Advice for drivers:

- Never drive if you are fighting sleep.

- Prepare yourself for driving by ensuring you get adequate sleep.

- If you are on any medication, check if it causes drowsiness.

- Prepare your journey properly, and plan where you can take a safe break from driving.

- Stop in a safe place when you feel tired.

- Drink a cup or two of strong coffee or a caffeinated drink and take a nap for a maximum of 20 minutes (set the alarm on your mobile phone). Caffeine takes about 20 minutes to take effect, so if you nap for more than 20 minutes, you might wake feeling groggy.

- After the nap, if it is safe to do so, get some fresh air and stretch your legs.

Note: these measures should only be considered in an emergency and should not be used on a regular basis. If you are a professional driver, you should consider what long-term steps you need to take which will help you to get the sleep that you need.

Do not be tempted to keep driving when you are tired because you are only minutes from your destination. Many tiredness-related collisions occur within a few minutes of the driver's destination as the body begins to relax.

For further advice and information on Driver Tiredness, see RSA leaflet 'Driver Tiredness' which is available to download on *www.rsa.ie*.

REMEMBER

If you are suffering from a serious lack of sleep, the only cure is sleep.

Road rage and aggressive driving

If you display road rage as a driver, it means you have uncontrolled anger that results in intimidation or violence against another driver.

Aggressive driving is inconsiderate, stupid driving. It can involve speeding, tailgating (driving too close behind another vehicle), failing to use an indicator for lane changes, recklessly weaving in and out of traffic and over-use of a horn or flashing headlights.

If another driver is attempting to provoke you, don't react. Don't be tempted to speed up, brake or swerve suddenly. This could cause a crash or make other drivers think you are confronting them. Instead, stay calm and remain focused on your driving to complete your journey safely. Always remember that safety is your number one concern.

Report all incidents to your local Garda station or contact Traffic Watch on: Lo-Call 1890 205 805.

Litter

Remember: Throwing litter from a vehicle is not only irresponsible but can cause a hazard to other road users and yourself.

> ### REMEMBER
>
> **It is an offence to supply a mechanically propelled vehicle to anyone who is under 16 years of age for use in a public place. Similarly, it is an offence to drive a vehicle whilst under age and without the necessary driving licence or learner permit. The word 'supply' means sell, hire, loan, gift or provide in any other way. If you do, you can be fined up to €5,000 or face up to six months' imprisonment.**

Section 14:

Correct behaviour at the scene of an accident

//

This section covers what you must do if you have been involved in an accident, whether with another vehicle, another user of the road and/or with an object along the road. It also outlines what to do if you come across an accident.

What drivers must do at an accident or in an emergency

- If you are involved in an accident, you must stop your vehicle and remain at the scene for a reasonable time. If anyone is injured or appears to need assistance, the driver of the vehicle must offer assistance. If vehicles are blocking the roadway or posing a danger to other road users, the roadway **should** be marked and the vehicle **should** then be removed as soon as possible.

- If you are asked by a Garda, you must give your name and address, the address where the vehicle is kept, the name and address of the vehicle owner, the vehicle's registration number and evidence of insurance, such as the name of your insurance company or a disc or motor insurance certificate. If there is no Garda at the scene, you must give this information to any person involved in the crash or, if requested, to an independent witness.

- If you or another person is injured and there is no Garda at the scene, the accident must be reported to the nearest Garda station.

If you fail to comply with the above requirements, with the intent of escaping civil or criminal liability, in situations where:

- you know someone has been injured and needs medical attention, or

- you know someone has been killed, or are reckless as to that fact,

you may be convicted and receive a fine of up to €20,000 or a prison term of up to 10 years.

- If the accident damages property only, and there is a Garda in the immediate vicinity, you **must** report it to the Garda. If there is no Garda available, you **must** provide this information to the owner or the person in charge of the property. If, for any reason, neither a Garda nor the owner is immediately available, you **must** give all relevant information at a Garda station as soon as reasonably possible.

> ### REMEMBER
>
> **Gardaí must conduct mandatory testing of drivers for alcohol at the scene of a crash where someone has been injured, or of a driver who has been injured and removed to hospital.**

- You are advised to keep a disposable camera with built-in flash in your vehicle, and, if possible, take photographs of the scene and any damage done.

- Take care when moving damaged or broken-down vehicles and make every effort to warn oncoming traffic of the accident.

- You can warn them by using your hazard lights.

- If you need to ask for another road user's help to warn traffic, do so right away.

- If you have a reflective advance-warning triangle, (heavy vehicles and buses **must** have one), place it on the road far enough from the scene of the accident to give enough warning to approaching traffic. A warning triangle **should not**, however, be used on a motorway or in a place where it would be unsafe.

- When placing a triangle, you **should** take account of prevailing road conditions, traffic speed and volume. This is particularly important on motorways and dual-carriageways.

- If the breakdown occurs near a bend in the road, make sure you give warning to traffic on both sides of the bend.

- Leaking fuel from a crashed vehicle is dangerous, so be careful approaching any vehicle after an accident.

- Carry at least two high-visibility vests or jackets and a torch in your vehicle. If there is an accident, wear the vest or jacket and use the torch to alert other road users of your presence.

What to do if you arrive at the scene of an accident

Dos ✓	Don'ts ✗
Do remain calm.	**Don't** panic – assess the situation before taking action.
Do switch off the engine and apply the handbrake.	**Don't** stay at the scene if there are enough people helping and keeping it under control.
Do use a reflective advance-warning triangle if available, except on a motorway.	**Don't** get injured yourself – park your vehicle safely out of the way.
Do switch on hazard warning lights and parking lights.	**Don't** move an injured person unless there is a risk of fire or of the vehicle turning over.
Do make sure you are safe as you try to help others.	**Don't** attempt to lift a car off an injured person without help.

Do make sure others are safe. You **should** keep any injured people warm, by placing coats or rugs around them.

Don't remove helmets from injured motorcyclists. Neck injuries are common in motorcycle collisions, and any attempt by inexperienced people to remove the helmet may leave the injured person paralysed from the neck down.

Do organise bystanders to warn oncoming traffic from both directions, if this has not already been done. Be particularly careful at night so that people giving help are visible (by wearing reflective armbands or bright clothes or carrying lit torches).

Don't allow anyone to smoke at, or close to, the scene.

Do call for help. Contact the emergency services on 999 or 112.

Don't give an injured person anything to eat or drink.

Accidents involving dangerous goods

If a vehicle carrying petrol, heating fuel or acid is in an accident, you **should**:

- keep well clear of the scene;
- position yourself, if possible, to make sure that the wind is not blowing from the accident towards you;
- warn other road users about the danger;
- give as much information as possible about the marking labels on the vehicle when summoning help; and
- let the emergency services do any rescuing.

The signs for vehicles carrying hazardous chemicals are shown below.

Harmful to skin　　*Explosive*　　*Bio Hazard*　　*Acid*

If you would like to know more about transporting dangerous goods by road, you can contact the Health and Safety Authority (*www.hsa.ie*) for a guide to the relevant domestic and EU laws governing this area.

Section 15:
Penalty points, fixed charges and driving bans

///

Encouraging good road user behaviour is important, and Ireland has adopted a system of penalty points to support this change. This system is a key part of road safety policy in this country, and is designed to save lives.

If you break the law, there's a price to be paid. The system will record your failure and the penalty on your driver licence record. For minor offences, the penalty is a sum of money, a fixed charge, and points that attach to your licence record: penalty points. For more serious offences you may be brought to court. The system applies to both full licence and learner permit holders.

If you break the law and are caught, you will be fined and you will build up penalty points.

> ### REMEMBER
>
> **A first-time learner driver (from 1 August 2014) who receives 7 points in a 36 month period will be banned from driving for 6 months.**
>
> **A novice driver (from 1 August 2014) who receives 7 points in a 36 month period will be banned from driving for 6 months.**
>
> **A fully licensed driver who receives 12 points in a 36 month period will be banned from driving for 6 months.**

This section describes how penalty points and fixed charges work and outlines the points and charges that apply to road traffic offences. For a list of all current penalty point offences and fixed charges, see Appendix 4 or *www.rsa.ie*.

Penalty points

The penalty points system covers offences that relate to road safety. Offences can be detected either:

- by Gardaí directly; or

- by safety cameras, in the case of speeding.

If a Garda stops you for committing an offence

- You must show your driving licence or learner permit, and give your name and current address, if asked.

- You will receive a fixed charge notice by post.

- You have the choice to pay the fixed charge within the time allowed (up to 56 days) or let the matter go to court.

- Penalty points will be applied to your licence record 28 days after the notification issues to you. This notification will be issued when you pay the fixed charge or, if applicable, when you are convicted of the offence in court.

If your vehicle is recorded breaking the speed limit

- If you are the registered owner of the vehicle, you will receive the fixed charge notice.

- If you were not driving the vehicle when the offence took place, you must give the Gardaí the name and address of the driver of your vehicle within 28 days. If you do, the named driver will receive the fixed charge notice. If you don't, you will be assumed to be the driver of the vehicle when the offence took place.

- Penalty points will be applied to the driver's licence record either when the charge is paid or when the driver is convicted of the offence in court.

> ### REMEMBER
>
> Most penalty point offences attract a fixed charge. Some offences will result in a mandatory court appearance without the option of only paying a fixed charge.

For more information on penalty points, visit the RSA website *www.rsa.ie* or *www.penaltypoints.ie*.

GET THE POINT! NOT THE POINTS!

Fixed charge system

This system applies to many offences, including most of the penalty point offences.

How it works

- You receive a fixed charge notice setting out:
  - the details of the offence;
  - the fixed charge amount to be paid; and
  - where that charge can be paid.
- You have 28 days to pay the fixed charge.
- If you do not pay the charge within this period, it increases by 50%. You then have another 28 days to pay the increased charge.
- If you do not pay it, the matter goes to court.

Driving bans

- If you build up 12 or more penalty points (as a fully licensed driver) or 7 or more penalty points (as a learner or novice driver from 1 August 2014) in 36 months:

  - you will receive a notice telling you that you have been banned from driving for 6 months from a particular date, and

  - you will have to post your driving licence to the NDLS within 14 days of the start of the driving ban.

- You will be banned from driving if you are convicted in court of an offence such as drink driving, dangerous driving or leaving the scene of a crash. You will be banned from driving as a result of the conviction alone, no matter how many penalty points are on your licence record.

- The courts can issue driving bans for any offences involving vehicles, not just the offences already resulting in automatic bans. The court will decide the period of the ban in each case.

- If you are convicted in court, you may be fined and, in some cases, face a prison term.

REMEMBER

It is an offence not to surrender your licence.

It is an offence to drive while banned from doing so.

Section 16:

Rules for motorcyclists

//

Motorcycles represent less than 1 in 50 of all licensed vehicles in Ireland, but motorcycle users account for 1 in 8 road deaths. In a crash, motorcycle and moped users have less protection than drivers or passengers in vehicles.

This section is aimed at motorcyclists, including those who use mopeds, and describes how you can keep yourself safe on the road. Trained motorcyclists around the world prove every day that biking can be a fun, safe and satisfying activity if you have appropriate skills, the right attitude to safety and the benefit of education and training.

Licence

You **must** hold a current driving licence or learner permit for a motorcycle or moped. See section 1 for information on licences and permits and the categories of vehicle they cover.

As a motorcyclist on a learner permit you will be required to display an 'L' on a yellow fluorescent tabard to give greater awareness to other road users that you are a learner and that additional care may be required. The 'L' **must** conform in size and colour to the normal 'L' plate.

If you have recently obtained your first driving licence (full driving licence) you will be classified as a 'Novice' driver and **must** display N plates on a yellow fluorescent tabard. This tabard **must** be worn over your clothes and the plates **should** be clearly visible on the front and rear of your body.

Insurance and tax

You **must** display a current motor tax disc and have insurance cover before you can take your motorcycle or moped on a public road.

Since December 2010 all new first time learner permit holders for motorcycles **must** undertake Initial Basic Training (IBT) with an approved IBT instructor, before they can ride a motorcycle unsupervised.

What is IBT?

Initial Basic Training (IBT) is a training course that teaches basic riding skills to learner motorcyclists. IBT is a 16-hour course broken into 4 modules focusing on theory and practical skills, to be taken in sequence.

When you have completed each IBT Module on your IBT course, your instructor will record the details of your training in your logbook and, once all modules have been completed, issue you with a Certificate of Satisfactory Completion.

You must keep your Certificate with your learner's permit and carry it with you whenever you are riding as you may be asked to produce it by a member of An Garda Síochána.

You can then apply for your practical driving test.

Carrying passengers

You must not carry a passenger if you hold a learner permit as this is illegal. If you wish to carry a passenger, make sure your full licence and your insurance policy allows you to do so. The rider must make certain the passenger is wearing a properly fitted crash helmet. The rider should make certain the passenger wears appropriate PPE (Personal Protection Equipment, that is, motorcycle jacket, trousers, gloves and boots – all properly fitting). A rider must not carry more than one pillion passenger, who must sit on a proper seat. They must face forward with both feet on the footrests. Riders must not carry a pillion passenger unless their motorcycle is designed to do so.

Daylight riding

- Make yourself as visible as possible from the side, as well as the front and rear.

- Wear a white helmet and fluorescent clothing or strips.

- Use dipped headlights. Even in good daylight, they may make you more visible.

Night-time riding

- Wear reflective clothing or strips to improve your chance of being seen in the dark. These reflect light from the headlamps of other vehicles, making you more visible from a long distance.

Lights

You **must** have on your motorcycle or moped:

- a white or yellow head lamp;

- a red rear lamp;

- a red rear reflector; and

- a number plate light on the back.

In order to be seen at all times it is important to:

- Use your dipped headlights at all times.

- Use headlights at night and during the day when visibility is seriously reduced.

- Slow down, and if necessary stop, if you are dazzled by oncoming headlights.

- Use full headlights when appropriate to do so.

- Use your hazard warning lights when your motorcycle or moped is stopped in a dangerous place.

- Make sure all sidelights and rear number plate lights are lit at night.

Personal protection equipment

Wear appropriate clothing and a secure helmet every time you get on your bike.

Protective clothes

- Jackets and trousers **should** give you enough protection from impact, abrasion, cold and weather conditions.

- Use body armour on exposed areas such as the back, knees, elbows, shoulders, hips and shins. This **should** be adjustable so it fits snugly and does not move in a crash.

- You **should** wear a good reflective jacket, to make you more visible on the road.

- Wear protective gloves, and footwear that comes above the ankle at least.

REMEMBER

It is a fixed charge offence of €80 to use a motorcycle without wearing a helmet or to permit a passenger to ride on a motorcycle without wearing a helmet.

Helmets

- Buy from reputable dealers. Try several different sizes and makes. Make sure the dealer knows how to assess fit.

- Never buy or use second-hand helmets.

- Never lend your helmet to someone else.

- If your helmet is damaged, replace it.

- Read the manual for your helmet and follow the care instructions.

- Clean your visor gently with warm soapy water.

- Use a helmet with a clear visor. If you use a dark visor, it will be almost impossible for you to see oil on a wet road.

- Replace the visor if it is scratched.

- Make sure your helmet is securely fastened. An unsecured helmet is illegal and useless in a crash.

- Do your research before you buy. Ensure all equipment meets EU standards.

Eye and ear protection

- Use ear protection on long journeys.

- If you wear an open-face helmet (one without a chin bar), make sure you wear eye protection.

- When riding a motorcycle, do not use a personal entertainment system.

Personal Protection Equipment

Without Protective Equipment | With Protective Equipment

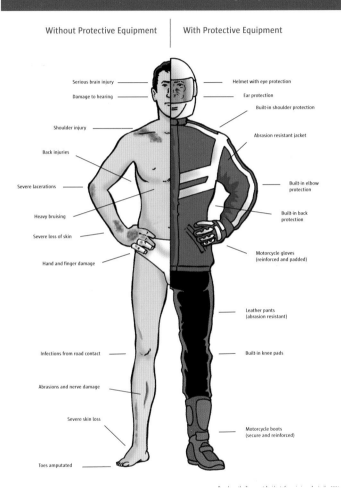

Serious brain injury — Helmet with eye protection

Damage to hearing — Ear protection

Built-in shoulder protection

Shoulder injury — Abrasion resistant jacket

Back injuries

Severe lacerations — Built-in elbow protection

Heavy bruising — Built-in back protection

Severe loss of skin

Hand and finger damage — Motorcycle gloves (reinforced and padded)

Leather pants (abrasion resistant)

Infections from road contact — Built-in knee pads

Abrasions and nerve damage

Severe skin loss

Motorcycle boots (secure and reinforced)

Toes amputated

Riding a motorcycle

As a motorcyclist you **must** obey the law governing traffic. You need to develop:

- a high level of attention;

- an awareness of likely hazards;

- good anticipation; and

- excellent observational skills.

You also need to make the most of the advantages of height, positioning, flexibility and manoeuvrability a motorcycle provides. The ability to sense danger in a situation develops only with experience, so you **should** always ride within your abilities.

Always make sure that the road space you intend to enter is completely safe, and be aware that others may be looking at larger objects and not the narrow profile of the motorcycle. Gravel chips, sand, pools of water and rough surfaces can seriously destabilise motorcycles and can be a cause of crashes. Reduce speed before hazards such as these, and continue riding with extreme caution.

Follow the rules below.

- Avoid riding between traffic lanes.

- Keep well clear of other vehicles when passing them. Remember that drivers might not always see you in their 'blind spots'.

- If your machine is fitted with indicators and a brake light, use them. However, if other road users cannot see these signals, or if you think they might not be working, you **should** give clear hand signals as well. See section 7 on hand signals.

- Use rear-view mirrors if your motorcycle or moped is fitted with them. Remember, though, not to rely on your mirrors when moving off, changing lane, turning right and overtaking. You **should** also look over your shoulders and check any 'blind spots'.

- Your motorcycle tyres **must** have a tread depth of at least 1 mm, but you **should** replace them before they become this worn.

Tactics for surviving as a motorcyclist

1. Watch your surroundings. This means watching:

    -   into the far, middle and near distance; and

    -   behind you, using your mirrors and checking over your shoulders, before changing position or turning.

2. Keep your distance. Use the 'two second rule' (see Section 8). In wet or icy conditions, always leave a bigger gap.

3. Be seen. Make sure your position is correct. Use dipped headlights and wear high visibility clothing (such as a neon vest and 'Sam Browne' reflective belt).

4. Do not surprise others. Never do anything on the road that could cause another road user to slow down, brake or swerve or that could startle pedestrians.

5. Think like other road users. Anticipate how other road users might react.

6. Read the road. In other words, ride to current road, weather and traffic conditions.

7. Adopt the right speed for the conditions. Never let others dictate your pace.

8. Never ride your bike after consuming alcohol or drugs.

9. Trust your machine by maintaining it properly. Follow the acronym **POWDERS** and check **p**etrol, **o**il, **w**ater, **d**amage, **e**lectrics, **r**ubber (tyres) and **s**ecurity.

You can get more detailed information on safety and on caring for and maintaining your motorcycle in the booklet *This is Your Bike* from the Road Safety Authority. Phone Lo-Call 1890 50 60 80, e-mail *info@rsa.ie* or visit the website *www.rsa.ie*.

Section 17:
Rules for cyclists

//

This section covers the rules for keeping your bicycle roadworthy, wearing proper equipment and cycling safely and considerately. You **must** also be familiar with the rules on cycle tracks (see pages 189–191) and hand signals (see Section 7).

Keeping your bicycle roadworthy

- Your brakes, tyres, chain, lights, reflector and bell **must** all be in good working order.

- Your bicycle **should** be the right size to allow you to touch the ground with both feet.

- When carrying goods, you **should** use a proper carrier or basket and take care that nothing is hanging loose.

- At night you **must** carry a lamp showing a white or yellow light to the front and a lamp showing a red light to the back. These are the minimum lighting requirements laid down by law. However, to be even more visible to motorists at night, you **should**:

  - add strips of reflective material to the bike (white to the front and red to the back);

  - wear a reflective armband; and

  - wear a 'Sam Browne' reflective belt or reflective vest.

> ### REMEMBER
>
> **Check your gear, be seen, wear a helmet and listen – never use mp3s, radios or mobile phones when cycling.**

Bicycle checklist

- Handlebars **should** be square with the frame and level with the saddle. Movement **should** be neither too stiff nor too loose.

- When on the saddle, both feet **should** just touch the ground.

- Your wheels **should** be straight and in line. Replace wheels if they are buckled or out of alignment.

- Tighten loose spokes and replace any that are damaged.

- Make sure your tyres are properly inflated, with a good tread.

- Make sure mudguards are secure and well clear of the wheels.

- Check your gears and get them adjusted when necessary.

- Check your brake cables and adjust them when necessary. Replace them when frayed.

- Make sure the closed ends of brake shoes face the front.

- Make sure brake blocks are close to the rim of the wheel. Replace worn blocks.

- Check pedals and replace them when worn or broken.

- Make sure your lamps are white or yellow to the front, and red at the back. Use a red reflector. Replace batteries when necessary and clean lenses.

- Make sure your bell is within easy reach of your thumb.
- Oil all moving parts.
- Wear a cycle helmet at all times.

A bicycle should have the following braking system:

- If it has one fixed wheel or is designed for a child under 7 years of age, it **should** have at least one brake.
- If it is designed for an older child or an adult, or if neither wheel is fixed, it **should** have two brakes – one brake acting on the front wheel and another for the back wheel.

Protective clothing and equipment

As a cyclist, you are a vulnerable road user and your bicycle will not protect you if there is a crash. The law does not require you to wear a helmet. However, in the interest of road safety, and in your personal interest, you **should** wear a helmet at all times.

When buying a helmet:

- Look for a mark to show that it has been made to a recognised national standard.
- Check that it does not restrict your field of vision or your hearing.

When you own a helmet you should:

- Replace it when it is damaged or dropped.
- Adjust the straps on your helmet to fit you correctly. Always check the manufacturer's instructions.

Cycling safely

- Make sure you keep to the left. Always look behind and give the proper signal before moving off, changing lanes or making a turn.

- You **must** obey the rules applying at traffic lights, pedestrian crossings, pelican crossings and zebra crossings.

- Keep both hands on the handlebars except when signalling or changing gears.

- Keep both feet on the pedals.

- Do not take up a position on the 'inside' of a large vehicle out of view of the driver. Instead, stay behind if the large vehicle has stopped at a junction with the intention of turning left.

- Keep clear of the kerb – riding clear will make you more visible and help reduce unsafe overtaking.

- When turning left, keep close to the left-hand side of the road, watch out for pedestrians and give the proper signal in good time.

- Beware of blind spots – all vehicles have blind zones and a driver may not be able to see you!

- When turning right, get into the centre or just left of centre of the right-turning lane. This helps to prevent a vehicle overtaking you whilst you are changing direction. Look behind and give the proper signal before you move out and ensure traffic in that lane is not going straight ahead. On steep hills or busy roads, pull into the left-hand side of the road and wait until there is a break in traffic in both directions to let you make the turn safely.

- When cycling alongside traffic stopped in line, be aware of gaps in the traffic to allow other vehicles to turn across the stationary lane. The view of the car that is turning may be blocked due to the traffic build-up.

- In poor weather conditions, or if you are not confident about taking up the position for turning right as outlined above, it may be safer to dismount and cross the roadway on foot. Where available, you should use a pedestrian or controlled crossing.

- Wear reflective clothing at all times.

In the company of one or more cyclists, you **must** have due regard to other users of the road, and you must take full account of prevailing road conditions. On occasion, it may be safe to cycle two abreast, but you **must not** cycle in a manner likely to create an obstruction for other road users.

Cycle tracks

A cycle **track** or **lane** is a reserved part of a roadway for bicycles (not motorcycles).

Some cycle tracks are bordered by a continuous white line on the right-hand side. These are only for bicycles and motorised wheelchairs, so no other drivers may use them or park in them.

Other cycle tracks have a broken white line on the right-hand side. Other drivers may make temporary use of this type of track if it is not occupied.

Cycle tracks are reserved 24 hours a day, unless an upright information sign at the start of or the side of the track shows another period of time.

A cycle track can also be a reserved part of a footpath or other area off the road.

If a cycle track is two-way, meaning bicycles travelling in opposite directions at the same time can use it, cyclists **should** stay as near as possible to the left-hand side of their track.

You **must** obey cycle track lights.

Rules on cycle tracks for other road users

Driving

No vehicle (other than a motorised wheelchair) may cross into or over a mandatory cycle track unless the driver is entering or leaving a place or a side road.

Parking

No driver may park a vehicle in a mandatory cycle track.

A driver may park in a non-mandatory cycle track for up to 30 minutes, but only if they are loading or unloading their vehicle and there is no alternative parking available. Remember the basic duty of care and do not obstruct a cycle track.

If a driver parks their vehicle in a cycle track that operates for only some of the day (shown on an information plate under the cycle track sign), they must move the vehicle by the time the next operating period starts.

If there is no information plate, it means the cycle track operates all the time and no parking is allowed.

Start of cycle track   End of cycle track   Information plate

The table below sets out particular road traffic rules on cycling which you **must** obey.

Dos ✓	Don'ts ✗
Do cycle in single file when overtaking.	**Don't** ever ride or attempt to ride a bicycle while under the influence of alcohol or drugs.
Do allow extra space when overtaking parked vehicles as the doors may open suddenly.	**Don't** ever ride on or across a footpath, other than where a cycle track is provided on the footpath.
Do cycle on cycle tracks where they are provided.	**Don't** ever hold on to a moving vehicle.
Do cycle in single file if cycling beside another person would endanger, inconvenience or block other traffic or pedestrians.	**Don't** ever cycle side-by-side with more than one cyclist.
Do cycle in single file in heavy traffic	**Don't** ever cycle against the flow of traffic on one-way streets.
Do give your name and address, if requested, to a Garda.	**Don't** ever cycle through red traffic lights or pedestrian lights.
Do obey signals given by a Garda or school warden.	**Don't** ever cycle on a motorway.
Do obey all rules applying to road traffic signs and road markings, including signs and signals at traffic lights, pedestrian crossings, pelican crossings, level crossings and zebra crossings.	**Don't** ever cycle in a contra-flow bus lane, unless signs authorise it.
Do know the meaning of hand signals for cyclists and use them when cycling.	**Don't** ever cycle without appropriate lighting during hours of darkness.

The table below lists the actions that you **should** take or avoid taking in the interests of your safety and that of other road users.

Dos ✓	Don'ts ✗
Do keep well back when cycling behind a motor vehicle in slow-moving traffic.	**Don't** ever hold on to or lean against stationary vehicles.
Do take extra care on wet or icy roads or when it is windy.	**Don't** ever weave in and out of moving traffic.
Do use your bell as a warning device only.	**Don't** ever carry a passenger unless your bicycle has been built or specially adapted to carry one.
Do take extra care and look well ahead for uneven road surfaces, drains and other obstructions so that you do not have to swerve suddenly in front of another vehicle.	**Don't** ever use a personal entertainment system when cycling.
Do use a bus lane, and be extra vigilant when a bus is stopped and about to move off from the stop.	**Don't** ever use a mobile phone while cycling.

Cyclists on roundabouts

- Be particularly careful when approaching a roundabout.

- Be aware that drivers may not see you easily.

- Watch out for vehicles crossing your path as they leave or enter the roundabout.

- Take extra care when cycling across exits.

- Give plenty of room to long vehicles on the roundabout, as they need more space. Do not ride in the spaces they need to use to get around the roundabout. Be aware of the driver's blind spots. If you can't see the driver, they can't see you. Indeed, it may be safer to wait until they have cleared the roundabout before you go on it.

Section 18:
Rules for pedestrians

//

Pedestrian deaths account for 1 in 5 deaths on our roads. This section covers the rules on walking along and crossing roads.

The most important rule for all pedestrians is to behave responsibly, exercise care and not endanger or inconvenience other users of the road.

Walking beside or along a road

- If there is a footpath, you **must** use it.

- If there is no footpath, you **must** walk as near as possible to the right-hand side of the road (facing oncoming traffic).

- Do not walk more than two abreast. If the road is narrow or carries heavy traffic, you **should** walk in single file.

- You **should** always wear bright and hi-viz clothing during the day and reflective clothing at night when walking outside built-up areas.

- You **should** always carry a torch when walking at night time.

- You **should** always be aware of other road users.

Crossing the road

Follow the DOs and DON'Ts below to make sure you cross the road safely.

Dos ✓	Don'ts ✗
Do look for a safe place to cross.	**Don't** cross at a corner or bend in the road.
Do stop and wait near the edge of the path. If there is no path, stand close to the edge of the road.	**Don't** cross near the brow of a hill.
Do look right and left and listen for traffic.	**Don't** cross near or at parked vehicles.
Do let any traffic coming in either direction pass, then look right and left again.	**Don't** cross where there are guard rails along the footpath.
Do walk briskly straight across the road when it is clear.	**Don't** hold onto or climb onto moving vehicles
Do continue to watch and listen for traffic while crossing.	**Don't** run across the road.

Taking care near buses or trams

Take extra care if crossing a road where there is a bus lane (especially a contra-flow bus lane), cycle lane or tram track. You **should** also be careful when getting on or off buses and when crossing the road at or near bus stops.

REMEMBER
Never cross in front of a stopped bus.

Safe crossing places

Use the following places to cross the road safely.

Zebra crossing

This is marked by yellow flashing beacons. The actual crossing area is marked by black and white 'zebra' stripes.

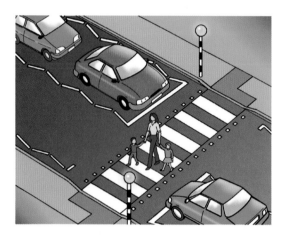

Drivers **must** stop to let you cross. As they approach the crossing, they **should** slow down and be prepared to stop. They **must** stop behind the stop line if there is one and **must** not enter any part of the crossing.

Drivers **must** not overtake or park within areas covered by zig-zag markings on either side of the crossing. Section 10, on parking, has more information.

- ○ You do not have the right-of-way over other traffic until you actually step onto the crossing. Never step onto the crossing if this would cause a driver to brake or swerve suddenly.

- ○ You **must** not cross within the area marked by zig-zag white lines if these are provided on either side of a zebra crossing. If they are not provided, you **must** not cross within 15 metres of the crossing.

- ○ If there is a central island, treat each side as a separate crossing.

- ○ Always watch carefully for approaching traffic. Place one foot on the crossing to indicate that you wish to cross. Wait until traffic has stopped before you start crossing.

Pedestrian lights

Pedestrian lights consist of a set of traffic lights for drivers and a set of light signals for pedestrians. Usually there is a push button for pedestrians. When you press it, the traffic lights will turn to red after a short while.

- Do not cross while the 'wait' or 'red man' light is showing.

- Cross with care when the 'cross now' or 'green man' is showing.

- If there is a central island at the pedestrian lights, the 'green man' or 'cross now' sign will let you cross only as far as that. You **must** then press the push button at another set of lights to cross the rest of the way.

- For vision-impaired pedestrians, an audible bleep signal and/or a vibrating panel on the push button may be in place to indicate when it is safe to cross.

Pelican crossing

At this crossing, an amber light will flash for a short period after the red light for drivers goes out. Similarly, the 'green man' light for pedestrians will flash for a short time before changing to the 'red man' light. A flashing amber light at a pelican crossing gives priority to pedestrians.

Traffic lights

If you are crossing at traffic lights, but there are no signals for pedestrians, check the lights in both directions. When the traffic on the road you wish to cross is governed by a red light, cross carefully. Look out for traffic that might be turning onto the road you wish to cross and remember that some traffic lights allow traffic to proceed in some lanes when other lanes are stopped. Be especially careful at junctions with filter lanes.

Uncontrolled crossing places

A traffic island is provided to help pedestrians. These are safer places to cross because the crossing is divided into two parts.

Don't cross the road in the area in front of a truck. This is a truck driver's blind spot.

> **REMEMBER**
>
> **If you can't see the driver, they can't see you.**

Section 19:
Respecting other road users

///

This section is aimed at motor vehicle drivers and builds on the information in Section 5 on good driving practice.

The vehicle does not have greater right of way than any other road user, so, for safety reasons, you **should** drive defensively. This means expecting the unexpected and making way for other road users when necessary.

Some of the actions you might need to take in normal conditions include:

- making way for an ambulance, fire engine or Garda vehicle;

- watching and stopping for children emerging from between cars; and

- waiting until a vehicle has started its left-hand turn before you emerge from a side road.

To make sure all road users are safe, be aware of your responsibilities towards:

- pedestrians, children, older people, people with disabilities and wheelchair users;

- cyclists and motorcyclists; and

- any animal traffic on the road.

This helps drivers to become safer and more socially responsible, not only to themselves, but to their families and other road users.

Pedestrians

As a driver, you **must not** put a pedestrian at risk. In particular, you **must** give way to pedestrians:

- on or at a zebra crossing (even if they are only waiting to cross);

- on or at a pelican crossing, when the amber light is flashing;

- crossing the road, if you are moving off from a stationary position (for example at a traffic light or a parking space); and

- at a junction, if they have started crossing the road.

Watch out for pedestrians who might attempt to cross the road suddenly from between parked vehicles. Make extra allowances for older people, people with disabilities and children. Watch for pedestrians walking to and from buses.

> ### REMEMBER
>
> **It is an offence to drive a vehicle partly or fully along or across a footpath, unless you are crossing a footpath to enter or leave a building or other place beside it.**

Children

By their nature, children have less experience than other people in using the road, so you **should** make extra allowances for their behaviour.

Take care when you are:

- driving beside footpaths where there are young children;

- coming out from side entrances or driveways;

- driving in car parks; and

- reversing, in particular where there are young children. You cannot see a small child behind your vehicle through your mirror. If in doubt, get out and check.

Schools

Do not park at a school entrance. Thoughtless parking can confuse parents and their children or block the entrance or exit of a school. It can also force children onto the road to get around your vehicle.

It is an offence if your vehicle blocks a footpath or a cycle track.

You **should** also take care near school buses, especially if overtaking a bus that children are boarding or leaving. School buses are clearly marked with stickers.

Do not leave any room for doubt. If you see school children, particularly young children, you may use your horn to let them know you are there.

Be careful near children who are cycling. Take extra care near a school, where cyclists may emerge in groups. Remember, it is hard to predict a young cyclist's balance and behaviour.

School wardens

Adult school wardens provide safe road crossing places for children outside or near schools. They wear a hat and an overcoat, which include reflective material. Wardens carry a special sign and are allowed by law to stop traffic.

When a warden raises the 'Stop' sign (shown below on the left), you **must** stop and remain stopped until:

- the school children have crossed the road;

- the sign is lowered; and

- the school warden has safely returned to the footpath.

Junior school wardens

Junior school wardens are the senior pupils of primary schools who operate in teams of six to give the same service given by an adult school warden. When they want traffic to stop, they give a signal to traffic on both sides of the road. When the traffic is stopped, the wardens take up their position and guide the younger children across the road. All vehicles **must** remain stopped until all the junior wardens have returned to the footpath.

Never park in a place that blocks a warden's view. School wardens **must** be able to see the road clearly to do their work properly and safely.

Cyclists and motorcyclists

Never put a cyclist or motorcyclist at risk and know your duty to be aware of them. They are especially vulnerable if there is a crash.

In particular, watch for cyclists and motorcyclists:

- at junctions;
- where cycle tracks merge with roads;
- when you change lanes;
- when opening your door to get out of a vehicle;
- when stopping and turning, especially when making a left turn; and
- when reversing.

The best way to take care near cyclists and motorcyclists is to use your mirrors and recheck blind spots.

Overtaking

Never cut in front of cyclists or motorcyclists when overtaking them. Give them plenty of space, especially:

- in wet or windy weather;
- when road conditions are icy;
- when they are starting off. Cyclists tend to wobble until they build up their speed; and
- when the road surface is poor. Cyclists and motorcyclists may need to avoid potholes.

Turning left

On left turns, watch out for cyclists and mopeds close to the kerb in front of you or coming up on your left. Do not overtake a cyclist as you approach a junction if you are turning left. The cyclist might be continuing straight ahead.

Turning right

When turning right through a gap in oncoming traffic (for example at a yellow box junction), watch out for cyclists who might be moving up on the inside (at the centre of the road) or might be travelling in a cycle or bus lane running in the opposite direction at the far side of the road. Also use your mirrors to check for any motorcyclists who may be overtaking you as you approach the turn.

Cycle tracks and parking

Do not park or drive on cycle tracks. Before you open the door of a parked vehicle, use your mirrors to check for cyclists and motorcyclists coming up on your right and give them enough room to pass.

Animal traffic

Always slow down and be prepared to stop when approaching or overtaking animals. If a person in charge of animals gives a signal to slow down or stop, you **must** obey it. Avoid using your horn if animals are in front of you, as it might frighten them.

If you are travelling on a road where animals are common, you will see a warning sign like the ones below.

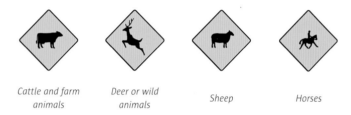

| Cattle and farm animals | Deer or wild animals | Sheep | Horses |

Section 20:

Other road users

///

Emergency services vehicles

In the course of their duty, Garda, fire brigade vehicles or ambulances and other emergency vehicles can be exempt from some of the road traffic law as long as this does not put other road users in danger. As a user of the road, if you hear or see a Garda or emergency vehicle approaching under emergency conditions and/or using a siren or flashing lights, you **should** exercise caution, and give way if it is safe to do so. Never 'tailgate' an emergency service vehicle (see pages 159–160).

People using agricultural machinery

Tractors

Tractors are governed by normal road traffic laws on driver licensing, insurance, motor tax and vehicle lighting.

All tractors used in a public place **must** be fitted with safety frames. The purpose of the frame is to protect the driver from being crushed underneath if the tractor overturns. The frame **must** comply with approved standards.

It is up to the owner or driver to fit a safety cab.

Tractors **must** carefully transport loose material such as silage, slurry, sand or gravel, so that the material does not spill onto a public road and cause a crash. Loads of lime or other dusty materials, offal or other offensive material **must** be fully covered with a tarpaulin.

Farmers using agricultural tractors and trailers to haul agricultural produce **must** not:

- use exceptionally high frames on trailers which could endanger the stability, steering and braking of an agricultural tractor and trailer combination; or

- exceed the maximum legally permissible combination weight or the design gross vehicle weight.

For more information contact the RSA on Lo-Call 1890 50 60 80.

Please note:
Further rules relating to various aspects of agricultural vehicles, such as lighting requirements, weight and dimension requirements, speed disc requirements, among others, will be implemented in 2016. Information on these new rules can be found on *www.rsa.ie* as it becomes available.

Tractors on the road

A tractor used in a public place **must** obey the laws governing road traffic.

If you are driving a tractor, you **should** keep left to let faster traffic pass. Your driving mirror **must** provide an adequate view of the road to the back.

Do not carry a passenger unless the tractor is equipped to carry one.

People in charge of animals

Horse-drawn vehicles

The normal rules apply, including the general rule to keep left. The hand signals to be given by the driver are the same as those given by a cyclist (see Section 7). A horse-drawn vehicle **must** be equipped with two red rear reflectors and, at night, **must** also carry on the right-hand side of the vehicle a lamp showing a white light to the front and a red light to the back.

You **must not** drive a horse-drawn vehicle while under the influence of alcohol or drugs.

Riding or leading horses

If you are riding or leading a horse, you **must** remain on the left-hand side of the road and obey all Rules of the Road.

You **should** wear a high-visibility vest and an approved riding helmet.

When leading a horse, you **should** walk ensuring the handler is between the horse and the traffic, so as to prevent the horse from interfering with the traffic.

When riding one horse and leading a second horse, you **must** remain on the left-hand side of the road. You **should** ensure the led horse is on the left-hand side of the ridden horse, to ensure the handler is positioned between the horse and the traffic. This is in order to control the led horse, in the interest of the safety of other users of the road.

*Accompanied
horses and ponies*

Drivers **should** take special care when:

- ⊙ approaching riding schools or places where horses are likely to appear.

- ⊙ overtaking horses, especially loose horses or horse-drawn vehicles.

- ⊙ approaching a horse and rider. If appropriate a driver **must** stop a vehicle and allow them to pass.

Driving animals on the road

If you are in charge of animals on a roadway, you **must** take reasonable steps to make sure the animals do not block other traffic or pedestrians.

If you are in charge of animals on the road at night, you **should** carry a lamp showing a white light to the front and a red light to the back. You **should** also wear a reflective armband.

Section 21:
Regulatory traffic signs

///

This section includes the signs that show a road regulation is in place. These must be obeyed.

Regulatory signs show the course a driver must follow and an action they are required to take or forbidden to take. They are generally circular and have a red border and black symbols or letters on a white background. Mandatory regulatory signs that indicate the direction traffic must take at junctions are blue and white.

| Stop | Yield | Yield | School wardens stop sign | No left turn |

| No entry or 'No straight ahead' | No right turn | Parking prohibited | Clearway | Max speed limit 30km/h |

| Max speed limit 50km/h | Max speed limit 60km/h | Max speed limit 80km/h | Max speed limit 100km/h | Max speed limit 120km/h |

The following is an alternative design for the 80km/h speed limit sign. This sign may be provided:

- on a local road to indicate that a speed limit of 80km/h applies; or

- at a location where special speed limit bye-laws specify that the special speed limit of 80km/h applies in respect of a local road or part of a local road in a built-up area.

*Max speed limit
80km/h*

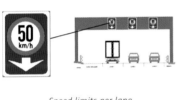

Speed limits per lane

No bicycles

*No ridden or
accompanied
horses*

*No entry to
vehicles*

*Maximum gross
weight (traffic
management)*

*Maximum vehicle
length*

*Maximum vehicle
width*

*Maximum axle
weight*

*No overtaking for
three-axle vehicles*

No horse carriages

Height restriction

Taxi rank

No entry for large vehicles (by reference to weight)

No U-turn

No overtaking

Height restriction

Maximum Gross Weight (Safety)

Pedestrianised street

Parking permitted

Disc parking plate

Zonal restriction – no parking of large vehicles

End of the restriction zone

Mandatory signs at junctions (white and blue)

Turn left ahead

Turn right ahead

Turn left

Turn right

Pass either side

Straight ahead

Keep right

Keep left

Manual traffic control sign at roadworks

No entry for pedestrians to tramway

Stop

Either form of Go or Téigh can be used

No entry to goods vehicles
(by reference to number of axles)

With flow bus lane on left | With flow bus lane on right | Contra flow bus lane | Tram lane on left | Tram lane on right

Start of cycle track | End of cycle track | Electronic variable speed limit sign (tunnel only) | Variable speed limit | In a tunnel goods vehicles cannot use right-hand lane *(by reference to number of axles)*

Electronic periodic speed limit sign | Electronic periodic speed limit sign at school | Tram only street | Tram and access only street | Bus only street

Turn back | Pedestrians and bicycles only | Separate bicycle and pedestrian lanes

Traffic lane control signs: tunnels, national roads and motorways

Go (Lane open)   Stop (Lane closed)   *Move into the left-hand lane*   *Move into the right-hand lane*

Variable message signs (VMS)

 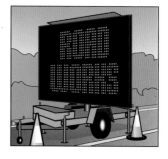

Overhead VMS   *Mobile VMS displaying text message*

 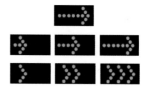

Mobile VMS displaying chevrons   *Examples of VMS chevron formats*

Section 22:
Warning traffic signs

///

This section includes signs that warn road users of a hazard ahead. They are diamond or rectangular in shape and have a black border and black symbols or letters on a yellow background.

Dangerous corner ahead

Roundabout ahead

Mini-Roundabout ahead

Merging traffic

Two-way traffic

Dangerous bend ahead

Series of dangerous bends ahead

Series of dangerous corners ahead

Restricted headroom

T-junction

Junction ahead with roads of less importance
(the latter being indicated by arms of lesser width)

T-junction

Y-junction

Side road

Crossroads

Junction ahead with a road or roads of equal importance

| Crossroads | Side road | T-junction | Y-junction | Staggered crossroads |

Advance warning of a major road (or dual carriageway ahead)

| T-junction with dual carriageway | Crossroads with dual carriageway | Crossroads |

General purpose warning signs

| Drive on left | Safe height plate | Low flying aircraft | Road divides |

| Merging/diverging traffic | Dual carriageway ends | Traffic cross-over ahead | Overhead electric cables |

| Traffic signals ahead | Pedestrian crossing ahead | Slippery road ahead | Road narrows on both sides |

| Road narrows from left | Road narrows from right | Tunnel ahead | Cyclists |

Start of a passing lane

Lane loss

Start of a climbing lane

Loop road ahead

Sharp dip ahead

Series of bumps or hollows ahead

Sharp rise ahead – for example, hump-back bridge

Deer or wild animals

Sheep

Cattle and farm animals

Accompanied horses and ponies

Crosswinds

Steep descent ahead

Steep ascent ahead

Danger of falling rocks

Unprotected quay, canal or river ahead

Low bridge ahead (height restriction shown)

Level crossing ahead, guarded by gates or lifting barrier

Level crossing ahead, unguarded by gates or lifting barrier

Level crossing ahead with lights and barriers

STOP
nuair a lasann
na
soilse dearga

STOP
When
Red Lights
Show

Stop when lights
are red

GO MALL
Crosaire
Comhréidh
Uathoibrioch

SLOW
Automatic
Level Crossing

Automatic level
crossing ahead

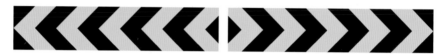

Chevron board
(a sharp change of direction to the left)

Chevron board
(a sharp change of direction to the right)

Warning signs for schools and children

School ahead

School children
crossing ahead

Aire Leanaí

CAUTION
CHILDREN

Children crossing
(in residential area)

Tram signs

Tram lane
crossing ahead

Féach gach treo
LOOK BOTH WAYS

Féach ar Dheis
LOOK RIGHT

Féach ar Chlé
LOOK LEFT

Tram lane warning signs for pedestrians

Tramrian
TRAM TRACK

Slippery for cyclists

Section 23:
Warning signs for roadworks

//

This section includes the warning signs for roadworks. Like other warning signs, these are diamond or rectangular in shape and have a black border and black symbols or text. However, they are orange in colour instead of yellow.

Roadworks ahead

One-lane crossover (out)

One-lane crossover (back)

Move to left (one lane)

Move to right (one lane)

Move to left (two lanes)

Move to right (two lanes)

Obstruction between lanes

End of obstruction between lanes

Start of central reserve or obstruction

End of central reserve or obstruction

Lanes diverge at crossover

Lanes rejoin at crossover

Two-lanes crossover (back)

Two-lanes crossover (out)

Single lane (for shuttle working)

Two-way traffic

Road narrows from left

Road narrows from right

Road narrows on both sides

| *Offside lane (of two) closed* | *Nearside lane (of two) closed* | *Offside lane (of three) closed* | *Nearside lane (of three) closed* | *Two offside lanes (of three) closed* |

| *Two nearside lanes (of three) closed. Two alternative styles* | *Offside lane (of four) closed* | *Nearside lane (of four) closed* | *Two offside lanes (of four) closed* |

| *Two nearside lanes (of four) closed* | *Side road on left* | *Side road on right* | *Site access on left* | *Site access on right* |

| *Temporary traffic signals ahead* | *Flagman ahead* | *Queues likely* | *Hump or ramp* | *Uneven surface* |

| *Slippery road* | *Loose chippings* | *Pedestrians cross to left* | *Pedestrians cross to right* | *Overhead electric cables* |

| Detour ahead | Detour to left | Detour to right | Road closed | Diverted traffic left |

| Diverted traffic | Diverted traffic | Diverted traffic | End of detour | Detour destination |

Information plates at roadworks

| Distance | Length | Direction | Direction and distance | End |

| Cautionary speed | Slow | Concealed entrance | Type of works | Use hard shoulder |

| Hard shoulder closed | Unfinished road surface | Barrier board | Chevron board | Speed limit ahead |

Manual traffic control sign at roadworks

| Flagman ahead | | Stop | Either form of Go or Téigh can be used |

Section 24:
Information signs

///

This section includes road signs showing directions and the location of services or other places of interest to tourists.

Advance direction signs

Motorway

National road

National road

Regional road

Lane destination sign

Direction signs (at junctions)

Motorway direction sign

National road direction signs

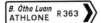

Regional road
direction sign

Regional road
direction sign

Local road direction sign

Destination distance sign

Town or village sign

Slow lane sign

Cul-de-sac

Industrial estate
symbol

Disabled persons
parking bay

Airport symbol

Ferry symbol

Alternative route
for high vehicles

Lay-by ahead sign

Hospital ahead
sign

Lay-by sign

Hospital sign

Car park with
facilities for disabled
persons

SOS lay-by

Speed camera

Advance information sign
for low clearance

Advance information sign
for low clearance

Alternative route for
heavy vehicles

Traffic calming sign   Traffic calming sign   Supplementary plate   Ramps on road

Tourist information signs

Advance sign for facilities in lay-by

Advance sign for lay-by with tourism information

Sign for Óige youth hostels

Advance direction to local services

Signing to approved tourist information

Tourist advanced direction sign

Tourist attraction direction sign

Pedestrian sign to a tourist attraction

Pedestrian sign to a car park

Sign to approved tourist information points

222

Section 25:
Motorway signs

///

These signs are rectangular with blue backgrounds and white writing or symbols.

Motorway ahead

Motorway ahead

Advance direction sign

Route confirmatory sign with Euro Route marker plate

Entry to motorway

300m to next exit

200m to next exit

100m to next exit

Motorway ends 1km ahead

Motorway ends 500m ahead

End of motorway

Route confirmatory sign for M7

Typical lane gain sign

Advance direction sign for destination

Typical 2km next exit sign

Appendix 1:
List of medical report requirements

//

If you have any of the diseases or disabilities listed below, you **must** supply a medical report when applying for a driving licence.

- Diabetes treated by insulin and/or sulphonylurea tablets. Ask your doctor whether you are on these or not. There is no need to report diabetes if managed by other tablets and/or diet.

- Epilepsy.

- Stroke or TIAs with any associated symptom lasting longer than one month.

- Fits or blackouts.

- Any type of brain surgery – brain abscess or severe head injury involving in-patient treatment – brain tumour, spinal injury or spinal tumour.

- An implanted cardiac pacemaker.

- An implanted cardiac defibrillator (ICD).

- Repeated attacks of sudden disabling dizziness.

- Any other chronic neurological condition, such as multiple sclerosis, motor neurone disease, Parkinson's disease or Huntington's disease.

- A serious problem with memory or periods of confusion.

- Persistent alcohol misuse or dependency.

- Persistent drug misuse or dependency.

- Serious psychiatric illness or mental health problems.

- Sleep apnoea syndrome.

- Narcolepsy.

- Any condition affecting your peripheral vision.

- Total loss of sight in one eye.

- Any condition affecting both eyes, or the remaining eye if you only have one eye (not including colour blindness or short or long sight).

- A serious hearing deficiency, which has worsened since your last application/renewal.

- Any persisting problem with arm(s) or leg(s) which needs driving to be restricted to certain types of vehicle, or those with adapted controls.

- Severe learning disability.

This list is not exhaustive. For further information on the medical report requirements, you can visit either *www.rsa.ie* or *www.ndls.ie*.

Appendix 2:
Laws covering road traffic and safety

//

This section lists the main laws on which the contents of this book are based. It divides the laws into Acts and regulations made under the Acts.

Acts

Road Traffic Acts

Road Traffic Act 1961

Road Traffic Act 1968

Road Traffic (Amendment) Act 1984

Road Traffic Act 1994

Road Traffic Act 1995

Road Traffic Act 2002

Road Traffic Act 2003

Road Traffic Act 2004

Road Traffic Act 2006

Road Traffic Act 2010

Road Traffic Act 2011

Road Traffic (No.2) Act 2011

Other relevant Acts

Local Authorities (Traffic Wardens) Act 1975

Road Acts 1920, 1993 and 2007

Finance Acts, 1960 and 1976

Finance (Excise Duties) (Vehicles) Act 1952

Dublin Transport Authority Act 1986

Dublin Transport Authority (Dissolution) Act 1987

Transport (Railway Infrastructure) Act 2001

Taxi Regulation Act 2003

Railway Safety Act 2005

Safety, Health and Welfare at Work Act 2005

Road Traffic and Transport Act 2006

Road Safety Authority Act 2006

Road Transport Act 2011

Motor Vehicle (Duties and Licences) Act 2012

Road Safety Authority (Commercial Vehicle Roadworthiness) Act 2012

Motor Vehicle (Duties and Licences) Act 2013

Non-Use of Motor Vehicles Act 2013

Taxi Regulation Act 2013

Road Traffic Act 2014

Road Traffic (No. 2) Act 2014

Regulations made under the Acts

Road Traffic (Construction, Equipment and Use of Vehicles) Regulations

Road Traffic (Construction & Use of Vehicles) Regulations

Road Traffic (Immobilisation of Vehicles) Regulations

Road Traffic (Courses of Instruction) (Learner Permit Holders) Regulations

Road Traffic (Licensing of Learner Drivers) (Certificates of Competency) Regulations

European Communities (Vehicle Testing) Regulations

Road Traffic (Traffic and Parking) Regulations

Road Traffic (Ordinary Speed Limits - Buses, Heavy Goods Vehicles, Etc.) Regulations

European Communities (Driving Theoretical Tests) Regulations

European Communities (Vehicle Drivers Certificate of Professional Competence) Regulations

Road Traffic (National Car Test) Regulations

Road Traffic (Special Permits for Particular Vehicles) Regulations

Road Traffic (Signs) Regulations

Road Traffic (Lighting of Vehicles) Regulations

Road Traffic (Registration and Licensing) Regulations

Road Traffic (Licensing of Drivers) Regulations

Road Traffic (Requirement to have Audible Warning Devices on Vehicles) Regulations

Road Traffic (Compulsory Insurance) Regulations

European Communities (Road Traffic) (Compulsory Insurance) (Amendment) Regulations

Road Traffic (Weight Laden of 5 Axle Articulated Vehicles) Regulations

Road Traffic (Insurance Disc) Regulations

Road Traffic Act, 1994 (Part III) Regulations

Road Regulations 1994

European Communities (Motor Vehicles UN –ECE Type Approval) Regulations

European Communities (Passenger Car Entry into Service) Regulations

European Communities (Road Transport) (Working Conditions and Road Safety) Regulations

European Communities (Mechanically Propelled Vehicle Entry into Service) Regulations

European Communities (Road Transport Activities Checks) Regulations

European Communities (Road Vehicles: Type-Approval) Regulations

European Communities (Road Vehicles: Entry into Service) Regulations

European Communities (Motor Vehicles Type Approval) Regulations

Road Traffic (Specialised Vehicle Permits) Regulations

Vehicle Registration and Taxation Regulations 1992

Road Traffic Act, 1994 (Section 17) Regulations 1999

Road Traffic (Ordinary Speed Limits – Certain Vehicles) Regulations 2005

Road Traffic (Speed Limit – Traffic Signs) Regulations 2005

Road Traffic (Traffic Signs – Periodic Special Speed Limits) Regulations 2005

European Communities (Installation and Use of Speed Limitation Devices in Motor Vehicles) Regulations 2005

European Communities (Compulsory Use of Safety Belts and Child Restraint Systems in Motor Vehicles) Regulations 2006

Road Traffic Act 2006 (Mobile Phones-Prescribed Numbers) Regulations 2006

Road Traffic Act 2002 (Commencement of Certain Provisions relating to Driving while Holding Mobile Phone) Order 2006

Road Traffic Acts 1961 to 2006 (Fixed Charge Offence) (Holding Mobile Phone While Driving) Regulations 2006

Road Traffic (Control of Traffic) Regulations 2006

Road Traffic Act 1994 (Control of Traffic - Exemption Permits) Regulations 2006

Road Traffic Acts 1961 to 2005 (Fixed Charge Offences) Regulations 2006

Road Traffic Act 2006 (Commencement) Order 2007

Road Traffic (Components and Separate Technical Units) Regulations 2007

Road Traffic (Components and Separate Technical Units) (Two and Three Wheel Motor Vehicle) Regulations 2007

Road Traffic (Recognition of Foreign Driving Licences) Order 2007

European Communities (Railway Safety) Regulations 2008

Road Traffic (Retreaded Tyres) Regulations 2008

Local Authorities (Traffic Wardens) Act 1975 (Fixed Charge Offences) Regulations

Road Traffic (Driving Mirrors-Requirements Vehicles) Regulations 2008

European Communities (Recognition of Driving Licences of other Member States) Regulations 2008

European Communities (Charging of Heavy Goods Vehicles for the Use of Certain Infrastructures) Regulations 2009

Road Traffic Acts 1961 To 2007 (Fixed Charge offences) (Prescribed Notice and Document) Regulations 2009

Taxi Regulation Act 2003 (Licensing of Dispatch Operators) Regulations 2009

Road Traffic (Driving Instructor Licensing) Regulations 2009

Road Traffic (Driving Instructor Licensing) (No. 2) Regulations 2009

Road Traffic Act 2006 (Part Commencement Section 16) (Penalty Points) Order 2009

Road Traffic Act 2002 (Commencement of Certain Provisions) (Penalty Points) Order 2009

Road Traffic (Display of Test Disc) Regulations 2009

Taxi Regulation Act 2003 (Small Public Service Vehicle Skills Development Programme and Driver Licence Fee) Regulations 2009

Roads Act 2007 (Declaration of Motorways) Order 2009

European Communities (Road Haulage and Road Passenger Transport Operator's Licences) Regulations 2009

Taxi Regulation Act 2003 (Licensing of Dispatch Operators) Regulations 2009

Railway Safety Act 2005 (Section 26) Levy Order 2010

Road Traffic Act 2002 (Section 9) (Commencement) Order 2010

European Communities (Commercial Vehicles Roadside Check Forms) Regulations 2010

Taxi Regulation Act 2003 (Wheelchair Accessible Hackneys and Wheelchair Accessible Taxis - Vehicle Standards) Regulations 2010

Taxi Regulation Act 2003 (Suitability Inspection and Annual Licence Renewal Assessment of Small Public Service Vehicles) Regulations 2010

Taxi Regulation Act 2003 (Grant of Taxi Licences) (Amendment) Regulations 2010

Taxi Regulation Act 2003 (Wheelchair Accessible Hackneys and Wheelchair Accessible Taxis - Vehicle Standards) (Amendment) Regulations 2010

Road Traffic Act 2010 (Certain Provisions) (Commencement) Order 2010

Road Traffic (Recognition of Foreign Driving Licences - New Zealand and Taiwan) Order 2010

Road Traffic Act 1994 (Section 17) (Prescribed Form and Manner of Statements) Regulations 2010

Road Traffic Act 1994 (Sections 18 and 19) (Prescribed Forms) Regulations 2010

Road Traffic Act 1994 (Section 22) (Costs and Expenses) Regulations 2010

Taxi Regulation Act 2003 (Suitability Inspection and Taxi Roof Sign) (Amendment) Regulations 2010

Public Transport Regulation Act 2009 (Certain Provisions) (Commencement) (No. 2) Order 2010

EC (Commercial Vehicles Roadside Check Forms)(Irish Language Form) Regulations 2011

Taxi Regulation Act 2003 (Vehicle Age Limit) (Amendment) Regulations 2011

Transport (Alteration of Name of Department and Title of Minister) Order 2011

Road Traffic (Courses of Instruction (Cars) Regulation 2011

Road Traffic Act 2011 (Commencement) Order 2011

Road Traffic Act 2010 (Certain Provisions) (Commencement) Order 2011

Road Traffic (Spray Suppression) Regulations 2011

European Communities (Carriage of Dangerous Goods by Road and Use of Transportable Pressure Equipment) Regulations 2011

Road Traffic (Restraint Systems in Organised Transport of Children) Regulations 2011

Road Traffic Act 2010 (Sections 15 and 17) (Prescribed Forms) Regulations 2011

Road Traffic Act 2010 (Section 13) (Prescribed Form and Manner of Statements) Regulations 2011

Road Traffic (No. 2) Act 2011 (Commencement) Order 2011

Road Traffic Act 2010 (Certain Provisions) (Commencement) (No. 2) Order 2011

Road Traffic Act 2010 (Section 33) (Commencement) Order 2011

Road Traffic Act 2010 (Fixed Penalty Notice - Drink Driving) Regulations 2011

European Communities (Random Roadside Vehicle Inspection) (Amendment) Regulations 2011

European Communities (End-of-Life Vehicles) (Amendment) Regulations 2011

Taxi Regulation Act 2003 (Vehicle Size and Wheelchair Accessible Vehicles) (Amendment) Regulations 2011

Road Traffic (Courses of Instruction) (Motorcycles) Regulations 2011

European Union (International Market for Coach and Bus Services) Regulations 2011

European Union (Occupation of Road Transport Operator) Regulations 2011

European Union (International Road Haulage Market) Regulations 2011

European Union (Motor Insurance) (Limitation of Insurance in relation to Injury to Property) Regulations 2011

European Communities (Road Transport) (Organisation of Working Time of Persons Performing Mobile Road Transport Activities) Regulations 2012

Light Railway (Regulation of Travel and Use) Bye-laws 2012

Roads Act 1993 (Classification of National Roads) Order 2012

Roads Act 1993 (Classification of Regional Roads) Order 2012

Railway Safety Act 2005 (Section 26) Levy Order 2012

Road Traffic Act 2010 (Section 48) (Commencement) Order 2012

Road Traffic Acts 1961 to 2011 (Fixed Charge Offences) Regulations 2012

Road Traffic Act 2006 (Part Commencement Section 16(2)(e) (Penalty Points) Order 2012

Road Traffic Act 2002 (Commencement of Certain Provisions) (Penalty Points) Order 2012

Road Safety Authority (Commercial Vehicle Roadworthiness) Act 2012 (Part 1 and Section 28) (Commencement) Order 2012

Road Traffic (Licensing of Trailers and Semi-Trailers) Regulations 2012

Road Vehicles (Registration and Licensing) (Amendment) Regulations 2012

Road Traffic Act 2010 (Section 21) (Costs and Expenses) Regulations 2012

Road Traffic (Licensing of Drivers) (Fees) Regulations 2012

Traffic Act 2010 (Section 53(3)(c)) (Commencement) Order 2012

Road Safety Authority (Commercial Vehicle Roadworthiness) Act 2012 (Part 3) (Commencement) Order 2013

Road Traffic (Licensing of Drivers) (Amendment) Regulations 2013

Road Traffic (National Car Test) (Amendment) Regulations 2013

Road Traffic Act 2002 (Certain Provisions) (Commencement) Order 2013

Road Traffic (Construction and Use of Vehicles) (Amendment) Regulations 2013

Taxi Regulation Act 2003 (Revised Vehicle Standards and Fixed Charge Offences) (Amendment) (Regulations) 2013

Road Traffic (Licensing of Learner Drivers) (Certificates of Competency) (Amendment) Regulations 2013

European Communities (Vehicle Testing) Regulations 2004 (Revocation) Regulations 2013

Road Safety Authority (Commercial Vehicle Roadworthiness) Act 2012 (Conferral of Functions) Order 2013

Road Safety Authority (Commercial Vehicle Roadworthiness) Act 2012 (Certain Provisions) (Commencement) Order 2013

Commercial Vehicle Roadworthiness (Vehicle Testing) Regulations 2013

Authorisation of Commercial Vehicle Roadworthiness Test Operators and Testers Regulations 2013

Disposal of Condemned Vehicles (Excise) Regulations 2013

Road Traffic (Signs) (Amendment) Regulations 2013

Road Traffic (Traffic and Parking) (Amendment) Regulations 2013

Non-Use of Motor Vehicles Act 2013 (Commencement) Order 2013

Non-Use of Motor Vehicles Act 2013 (Commencement) (No. 2) Order 2013

Non-Use of Motor Vehicles Regulations 2013

Road Traffic (Licensing of Drivers) (Amendment) (No. 2) Regulations 2013

European Communities (Carriage of Dangerous Goods by Road and Use of Transportable Pressure Equipment) (Amendment) Regulations 2013

Road Traffic (National Car Test) (Amendment) (No. 2) Regulations 2013

Road Transport Operator Licensing (Fees) Regulations 2013

Non-Use of Motor Vehicles (Section 3) Regulations 2013

European Union (End-of-Life Vehicles) (Amendment) Regulations 2013

Road Vehicles (Registration and Licensing) (Amendment) Regulations 2013

European Communities (Vehicle Drivers Certificate of Professional Competence) (Amendment) Regulations 2013

Commercial Vehicle Roadworthiness (Vehicle Testing) (No. 2) Regulations 2013

Road Safety Authority (Commercial Vehicle Roadworthiness) (Vehicle Maintenance and Repair) Regulations 2013

Road Safety Authority (Commercial Vehicle Roadworthiness) Act 2012 (Sections 30, 31 and 39) (Commencement) Order 2013

Taxi Regulation Act 2003 (Vehicle Licensing and Standards) (Amendment) Regulations 2013

European Communities (Agricultural or Forestry Tractors Type Approval) (Amendment) Regulations 2013

European Communities (Control of Emissions of Gaseous and Particulate Pollutants from Non-Road Mobile Machinery) (Amendment) Regulations 2013

Road Traffic (Licensing of Drivers) (Amendment) (No. 3) Regulations 2013

Vehicle Registration (Identification Marks) Regulations 2013

Taxi Regulation Act 2003 (Local Area Hackney) Regulations 2013

Road Traffic (Licensing of Drivers) (Amendment) (No. 4) Regulations 2013

European Communities (Road Vehicles: Type-Approval) (Amendment) Regulations 2013

European Communities (Mechanically Propelled Vehicle Entry into Service) (Amendment) Regulations 2013

European Communities (Motor Vehicles Type Approval) (Amendment) Regulations 2013

European Communities (Two and Three Wheel Motor Vehicle Entry into Service) (Amendment) Regulations 2013

European Communities (Road Vehicles: Entry into Service) (Amendment) Regulations 2013

Taxi Regulation Act 2013 (Public Service Contracts) (Commencement) Order 2013

Disabled Drivers and Disabled Passengers (Tax Concessions) (Amendment) Regulations 2014

Road Traffic Act 2014 (Certain Provisions) (Commencement) Order 2014

Taxi Regulation Act 2013 (Commencement) Order 2014

Small Public Service Vehicle (Consolidation and Reform) Regulations 2014

Road Traffic (Construction and Use of Vehicles) (Amendment) Regulations 2014

Road Traffic Act 2006 (Restriction on Use of Mobile Phones) Regulations 2014

European Communities (Motor Vehicles Type Approval) (Amendment) Regulations 2014.

European Communities (Two and Three Wheel Motor Vehicle Entry into Service) (Amendment) Regulations 2014

Road Vehicles (Registration and Licensing) (Amendment) Regulations 2014

Road Traffic (Plating and Speed Rating of Agricultural Vehicles) Regulations 2014

Road Traffic (Construction, Equipment and Use of Vehicles) (Amendment) Regulations 2014

Road Traffic (Lighting of Vehicles) (Amendment) Regulations 2014

Road Traffic (Construction and Use of Vehicles) (Amendment) (No. 2) Regulations 2014

European Union (End-of-Life Vehicles) Regulations 2014

Road Transport Operator Licensing (Fees) Regulations 2014

Road Traffic (National Car Test) Regulations 2014

Road Traffic (Traffic and Parking) (Car Clubs and Electrically Powered Vehicles) Regulations 2014

Road Traffic (Licensing of Drivers) (Amendment) Regulations 2014

Road Traffic (Signs) (Amendment) Regulations 2014

Road Traffic Act 2014 (Section 10(a) and (f)) (Commencement) Order 2014

Road Traffic (Licensing of Drivers) (Amendment) (No. 2) Regulations 2014

Road Traffic Act 2014 (Sections 1 and 2) (Commencement) Order 2014

European Union (Charging of Heavy Goods Vehicles for the Use of Certain Infrastructures) (Amendment) Regulations 2014

Commercial Vehicle Roadworthiness (Vehicle Licensing) Regulations 2014

European Union (Paints, Varnishes, Vehicle Refinishing Products and Activities) (Amendment) Regulations 2014

Road Traffic (Recognition of Foreign Driving Licences) (Ontario) Order 2014

European Communities (Driving Theoretical Tests) (Amendment) Regulations 2014

European Communities (Vehicle Drivers Certificate of Professional Competence) (Amendment) Regulations 2014

Road Traffic (Speed Limit - Traffic Signs) (Local Roads) Regulations 2014

Road Traffic Acts 1961 to 2014 (Small Public Service Vehicle) (Fixed Charge Offences) Regulations 2014

Road Safety Authority (Commercial Vehicle Roadworthiness) Act 2012 (Commencement) (Penalty Points - Certificate of Road Worthiness) Order 2014

Road Vehicles (Registration and Licensing) (Amendment) Regulations 2014

European Communities (Agricultural or Forestry Tractors Type Approval) (Amendment) Regulations 2014

Road Traffic Act 2010 (Impairment Testing) Regulations 2014

Road Traffic Act 2014 (Sections 12 and 13) (Commencement) Order 2014

Road Traffic Act 2010 (Impairment Testing) (Commencement) Order 2014

Road Traffic (Fixed Charge Offences) Regulations 2014

Road Traffic Act 2006 (Commencement) (Penalty Point - Speed Limitation Devices) Order 2014

Road Traffic Act 2014 (Section 10 (a) to (e) and (h)) (Commencement) Order 2014

Road Traffic (Weight Laden of 5 Axle Articulated Vehicles) Regulations 2014

Disposal of Condemned Vehicles (Excise) Regulations 2014

Taxi Regulation (Small Public Service Vehicle) Regulations 2015

European Communities (Road Transport) (Organisation of Working Time of Persons Performing Mobile Road Transport Activities) (Amendment) Regulations 2015

National Vehicle and Driver File (Access) Regulations 2015

European Union (Occupation of Road Transport Operator) Regulations 2015

Appendix 3:

Useful websites

///

Driving tests and theory tests

Driver Theory Test   *www.theorytest.ie*

Driving Test   *http://www.rsa.ie/RSA/Learner-Drivers/*
                            The-Driving-Test/Apply-online/

Information on the driving test   *www.rsa.ie*

Information on driving licensing   *www.ndls.ie*

Safety

Road Safety Authority   *www.rsa.ie*

Health and Safety Authority   *www.hsa.ie*

National Roads Authority   *www.nra.ie*

Penalty points

Penalty points   *www.penaltypoints.ie*

Vehicle testing

National Car Test   *www.ncts.ie*

Vehicle registration

Information on registration plates   *www.revenue.ie*

Government bodies

Luas	*www.luas.ie*
Dublin Port Tunnel	*www.dublinporttunnel.ie*
National Roads Authority (NRA)	*www.nra.ie*
Department of the Environment, Community and Local Government	*www.environ.ie*
Department of Transport, Tourism and Sport	*www.dttas.ie*
Department of Education and Skills	*www.education.ie*
Revenue Commissioners	*www.revenue.ie*
An Garda Síochána	*www.garda.ie*
Railway Safety Commission	*www.rsc.ie*
Iarnród Éireann	*www.irishrail.ie*

Weather services

Met Éireann	*www.met.ie*

Appendix 4:

Penalty points and fixed charge offences

//

Table 1: Offences incurring Penalty Points and Fixed Charge Notices with effect from December 2014

'm' means a mandatory court appearance

Offences incurring penalty points	Penalty points on payment	Penalty points on conviction	Amount paid in 28 days	Amount paid in next 28 days
Learner permit holder driving unaccompanied by qualified person	2	4	80	120
Failure to display N-plate or tabard	2	4	60	90
Failure to display L-plate or tabard	2	4	60	90
Contravention of ban on U-turns	2	4	60	90
Contravention of rules for use of mini-roundabouts	1	3	60	90
Proceeding beyond no entry to vehicles sign	1	3	60	90
Proceeding beyond a traffic lane control sign other than in accordance with such sign or without yielding	1	3	60	90
Using vehicle in a public place without an authorisation plate	3	5	60	90
Using vehicle in a public place that has been modified or altered such that authorisation plate is inaccurate	3	5	60	90

'm' means a mandatory court appearance

Offences incurring penalty points	Penalty points on payment	Penalty points on conviction	Amount paid in 28 days	Amount paid in next 28 days
Using vehicle not equipped with a speed limitation device or using a vehicle equipped with a speed limitation device not complying with requirements specified in Regulations	3	5	60	90
Proceeding beyond maximum vehicle length sign where length exceeds maximum displayed	1	3	60	90
Proceeding beyond maximum vehicle width sign where width exceeds maximum displayed	1	3	60	90
Proceeding beyond maximum design gross vehicle weight (safety) sign where design gross vehicle weight exceeds maximum displayed	1	3	60	90
Proceeding beyond maximum vehicle axle loading weight sign where vehicle axle loading weight exceeds maximum specified	1	3	60	90
Using vehicle (car) without test certificate (NCT)	3	5	60	90
Holding a mobile phone while driving	3	5	60	90
Dangerous overtaking	3	5	80	120
Failure to stop a vehicle before stop sign/stop line	3	5	80	120
Failure to yield right of way at a yield sign/yield line	3	5	80	120
Crossing continuous white line	3	5	80	120
Failure by vehicle to obey traffic lights	3	5	80	120
Failure to drive on the left hand side of the road	2	4	60	90
Contravention of prohibition of driving vehicle along or across median strip i.e. the boundary between two carriageways	2	4	60	90

Fixed charge €

'm' means a mandatory court appearance

			Fixed charge €	
Offences incurring penalty points	Penalty points on payment	Penalty points on conviction	Amount paid in 28 days	Amount paid in next 28 days
Failure to stop for school warden sign	2	5	80	120
Failure to leave appropriate distance between you and the vehicle in front	3	5	80	120
Failure to comply with mandatory traffic signs at junctions	2	4	80	120
Parking a vehicle in a dangerous position	3	5	80	120
Speeding	3	5	80	120
Driver of car or goods vehicle not wearing safety belt	3	5	60	90
Failure by Driver to comply with rear seat belt requirements for passengers under 17 years of age	3	5	60	90
Driver of car or goods vehicle permitting child under 3 years of age to travel in it without being restrained by appropriate child restraint	3	5	60	90
Driver of car or goods vehicle permitting child over 3 years of age to travel in it without being restrained by appropriate child restraint	3	5	60	90
Driver of car or goods vehicle permitting child to be restrained by rearward facing child restraint fitted to a seat protected by active frontal air-bag	3	5	60	90
Driver of bus not wearing safety belt	3	5	60	90
Driving vehicle before remedying dangerous defect	m	3	Court fine	
Driving dangerously defective vehicle	m	5	Court fine	
Using commercial vehicle without certificate of roadworthiness	m	5	Court fine	

'm' means a mandatory court appearance

Offences incurring penalty points	Penalty points on payment	Penalty points on conviction	Amount paid in 28 days	Amount paid in next 28 days
Bridge strikes, etc.	m	3	Court fine	
Failure to act in accordance with a Garda signal	1	3	80	120
Entry by driver into hatched marked area of roadway, for example, carriageway reduction lane	1	3	80	120
Failure by driver of vehicle to obey traffic rules at railway level crossing, swing bridge or lifting bridge	2	5	80	120
Driving a vehicle on a motorway against the flow of traffic	2	4	80	120
Driving on the hard shoulder on a motorway	1	3	80	120
Driving a vehicle (subject to an ordinary speed limit of 90 km/h or less) on the outside lane on a motorway	1	3	80	120
Failure to obey requirements at junctions, for example, Not being in the correct lane when turning onto another road	1	3	60	90
Failure to obey requirements regarding reversing of vehicles, for example, Reversing from minor road onto main road	1	3	60	90
Driving on a footpath	1	3	60	90
Driving on a cycle track	1	3	60	90
Failure to turn left when entering a roundabout	1	3	60	90
Failure to stop when so required by a member of the Garda Síochána	2	5	80	120
Failure by driver of vehicle to yield right of way	2	4	80	120

'm' means a mandatory court appearance

Fixed charge €

Offences incurring penalty points	Penalty points on payment	Penalty points on conviction	Amount paid in 28 days	Amount paid in next 28 days
Driving without reasonable consideration	2	4	80	120
Failure to comply with prohibitory traffic signs	1	3	60	90
Failure to comply with keep left/keep right signs	1	3	60	90
Failure to comply with traffic lane markings	1	3	60	90
Illegal entry onto a one-way street	1	3	60	90
Driving a vehicle when unfit	m	3	Court fine	
Breach of duties at an accident	m	5	Court fine	
Driving without insurance	m	5	Court fine	
Using vehicle – (a) whose weight un-laden exceeds maximum permitted weight, (b) whose weight laden exceeds maximum permitted weight, or (c) any part of which transmits to ground greater weight than maximum permitted weight	1	3	200	300
Driver found to be driving carelessly	m	5	Court fine	
Drink Driving Offences(In all cases where the BAC is between 50 mg and 80 mg of alcohol per 100 millilitres of blood)	3	n/a	200	

12 penalty points = **Automatic Disqualification**
7 penalty points = **Automatic Disqualification**, where the person was first issued with a learner permit on or after 1 August 2014, during the period the person drives under a learner permit and during the first two years while the person drives under a first full driving licence

Table 2 – Traffic offences included in the fixed charge system since 3 August 2012

General description of offense	Fixed charge €	
	If paid within 28 days	If paid within a further 28 days
Using motor cycle without wearing crash helmet	80	120
Permitting passenger not wearing crash helmet to be carried on motor cycle	80	120
Using vehicle not equipped with prescribed lamps and identification mark lighting	60	90
Using trailer not equipped with prescribed lamps and identification mark lighting	60	90
Using vehicle not equipped with prescribed rear projecting load lamp or lateral projecting load lamp	60	90
Using trailer not equipped with prescribed marker lamp	60	90
Using public service vehicle not equipped with prescribed internal lighting	60	90

Appendix 5:

Representative vehicles for the driving test

//

Since January 2013, there are significant changes to the types of vehicles that can be used in the practical driving test. You will see the details of these changes on your appointment letter and in RSA driving test centres. You can also visit *www.rsa.ie* for further information. The following tables show details of the vehicles that **can** be used for driving tests from 30 November 2013.

	AM	Two-wheeled or three-wheeled, other than with twinned wheels, mechanically propelled vehicle, not capable of being manually propelled. The machine must have a cylinder capacity not exceeding 50cm³, in the case of an internal combustion engine, or a maximum continuous rated power of no more than 4 kilowatts in the case of an electric motor. The vehicle must have a design speed of at least 25km/h but not more than 45km/h.
	A1	A Category A1 motorcycle, other than with twinned wheels, without sidecar, with a cylinder capacity of at least 115cm³ and not exceeding 125cm³, and capable of a speed of at least 90km/h, with an engine power not exceeding 11kW and with a power/weight ratio not exceeding 0.1kW/kg. If the motorcycle is powered by an electric motor, the power to weight ratio of the vehicle shall be at least 0.08kW/kg.
	A2	A Category A2 motorcycle, other than with twinned wheels, without sidecar, with a cylinder capacity of at least 395cm³, and an engine power of at least 20kW, but not exceeding 35kW, and with a power/weight ratio not exceeding 0.2kW/kg, and not derived from a vehicle of more than double its power. If the motorcycle is powered by an electric motor, the power to weight ratio of the vehicle shall be at least 0.15kW/kg.
	A	A Category A motorcycle, other than with twinned wheels, without sidecar, with a cylinder capacity of at least 595cm³, an unladen mass of more than 175kg, and an engine power of at least 50kW. If the motorcycle is powered by an electric motor, the power to weight ratio of the vehicle shall be at least 0.25kW/kg.

B

Four-wheeled vehicles (for example, cars/light vans), having a maximum authorised mass not exceeding 3,500kg, with passenger accommodation for not more than 8 persons and capable of a speed of at least 100km/h.

BE

A combination, made up of a Category B test vehicle which should be either (a) a length of at least 4.25 metres, or (b) a 4 wheel drive vehicle and a trailer with a maximum authorised mass of between 1,400–3,500 kg, capable of a speed of at least 100km/h, which does not fall within Category B. The cargo compartment of the trailer must consist of a permanent, closed box body which is at least as wide and as high as the motor vehicle, and at least 2.4 metres long. The closed box body may be slightly less wide than the motor vehicle, provided that the view to the rear is only possible by use of the external rear-view mirrors of the motor vehicle. The trailer must be presented with a real total mass (the actual weight of the trailer including the necessary load) of at least 800kg, having due regard for safety, stability, manufacturer's guidelines and legal limits of the combination.

In order to meet the Real Total Mass requirement you are required to place 30 four inch (100 X 220 X 450mm) solid concrete blocks in the trailer. The blocks should be evenly distributed across the trailer and positioned in such a way as to keep the nose weight within recommended limits.

C1

Vehicles (larger vans/light trucks) with passenger accommodation for not more than 8 persons, a maximum authorised mass of at least 4,000kg, but not more than 7,500kg, a length of at least 5 metres and capable of a speed of at least 80km/h. The vehicle must be fitted with anti-lock brakes and recording equipment (tachograph). The cargo compartment shall consist of a permanently mounted cube shaped closed box body, which is at least as wide and as high as the cab.

C

Vehicles (rigid trucks) with passenger accommodation for not more than 8 persons, a maximum authorised mass of at least 12,000kg, a length of at least 8 metres, a width of at least 2.4 metres, capable of a speed of at least 80km/h.

The vehicle must be fitted with anti-lock brakes, be equipped with a gearbox having at least 8 forward ratios and providing for a manual selection of gears by the driver, and with recording equipment (tachograph). A Cyclops mirror must be fitted where required. The cargo compartment shall consist of a permanently mounted cube shaped closed box body, which is at least as wide and as high as the cab. The vehicle must be presented with a real total mass (the actual weight of the vehicle including any load if necessary) of at least 10,000kg, having due regard for safety, stability, manufacturer's guidelines and legal limits.

C1E

A combination made up of a Category C1 test vehicle, and a trailer with a maximum authorised mass of at least 2,000kg. The combination must be at least 8 metres in length, and must be capable of a speed of at least 80km/h. The combination must have a maximum authorised mass of not more than 12,000kg, and the gross vehicle weight of the trailer must not exceed the unladen weight of the drawing vehicle.

The cargo compartment of the trailer must consist of a permanent, closed box body which is at least as wide and as high as the cab, and have a length of at least 2.4 metres. The closed box body may also be slightly less wide than the cab, provided that the view to the rear is only possible by use of the external rear-view mirrors of the motor vehicle. The trailer must be presented with a real total mass (the actual weight of the trailer including the necessary load) of at least 800kg, having due regard for safety, stability, manufacturer's guidelines and legal limits of the combination.

CE

Either (a) an articulated vehicle, or (b) a combination of a Category C test vehicle and a trailer of at least 7.5 metres in length. Both the articulated vehicle and the combination must have passenger accommodation for not more than 8 persons, at least 4 axles, a maximum authorised mass of at least 20,000 kg, a length of at least 14 metres, a width of at least 2.4 metres and be capable of a speed of at least 80 km/h.

The vehicle must be fitted with anti-lock brakes, be equipped with a gearbox having at least 8 forward ratios and providing for a manual selection of gears by the driver, and with recording equipment (tachograph). A Cyclops mirror must be fitted where required. The cargo compartment shall consist of a permanently mounted cube shaped closed box body which is at least as wide and as high as the cab. The articulated vehicle or the combination must be presented with a real total mass (the actual weight of the combination including any load if necessary) of at least 15,000kg, having due regard for safety, stability, manufacturer's guidelines and legal limits of the combination.

D1

Vehicles (minibuses) having passenger accommodation for more than 8 persons, but not more than 16 persons, a maximum authorised mass of at least 4,000kg, a length of at least 5 metres and capable of a speed of at least80km/h. The vehicle must be fitted with anti-lock brakes, and recording equipment (tachograph).

D

Vehicles (buses) having passenger accommodation for more than 16 persons, a length of at least 10 metres, a width of at least 2.4 metres and capable of a speed of at least 80km/h. The vehicle must be fitted with anti-lock brakes and recording equipment (tachograph).

![D1E icon]	**D1E**	A combination made up of a Category D1 test vehicle, and a trailer with a maximum authorised mass of at least 1,400kg, capable of a speed of at least 80km/h. The cargo compartment of the trailer must consist of a permanent, closed box body which is at least 2 metres wide, 2 metres high, and have a length of at least 2.4 metres. The combination must have a gross vehicle weight of not more than 12,000kg, and the gross vehicle weight of the trailer must not exceed the unladen weight of the drawing vehicle . The trailer must be presented with a real total mass (the actual weight of the trailer including the necessary load) of at least 800kg, having due regard for safety, stability, manufacturer's guidelines and legal limits of the combination.
![DE icon]	**DE**	A combination made up of a Category D test vehicle, and a trailer with a maximum authorised mass of at least 1,400 kg, capable of a speed of at least 80km/h. The cargo compartment of the trailer must consist of a permanent, closed box body which is at least 2 metres wide, 2 metres high, and has a length of at least 2.4 metres. The trailer must be presented with a real total mass (the actual weight of the trailer including any load if necessary) of at least 800kg, having due regard for safety, stability, manufacturer's guidelines and legal limits of the combination.
![W icon]	**W**	Works vehicles and land tractors.

Glossary

///

Abreast	Side by side
Acceleration	Speeding up
Arrhythmia	Irregular or abnormal heart beat
Axle	A pin, pole, or bar that connects a pair of opposite wheels on a vehicle
Blind spot	An area that a driver or other road user cannot see directly or with their mirrors. This requires them to turn or look sideways to see other road users
Blow out	Sudden tyre failure
Build outs	Kerbing which extends from the side of the road to reduce traffic speed
Cardiovascular diseases	Diseases involving the heart and blood system
Central median island	An area in the centre of a road which separates approaching flows of traffic or a pedestrian crossing
Central nervous system	Brain and spinal cord
Cerebrovascular diseases	Diseases involving blood vessels in the brain
Certificate of Professional Competency (CPC)	A certificate drivers must have before they can drive a HGV or a bus for a living
Chicane	A traffic-calming measure to make vehicles slow down and weave between traffic lanes
Chevron board	Traffic warning signs with hatched markings indicating a sudden change in direction
Cross-ply tyres	Tyres with cords made of steel and other materials, which cross at various angles to strengthen the side of the tyre and its tread
Deceleration	Slowing down
Defects	Faults, such as broken mirrors, missing lights
Design Gross Vehicle Weight (DGVW)	The manufacturers specifications of Gross Vehicle Weight (GVW see below)
Diverging	Moving apart. For example, traffic taking a right turn when other traffic is moving straight ahead or traffic leaving a motorway

Fixed-wheel bicycle	A bicycle you can back-pedal to brake. It has one wheel which cannot rotate independently of the pedals
Gantries	Overhead steel structures across carriageways to hold up signs
Garda Síochána	Ireland's national police service
Ghost island	A marked area on the road that shows where a motorway and a slip road meet
Graduating	Moving from one stage to the next
Gross vehicle weight (GVW)	The weight of a vehicle together with the maximum load it is designed to carry
Hard shoulder	A part of the road that is divided by broken or continuous yellow lines from the rest of the road and **should** be used only by certain road users in certain situations
Hatched marking	Chevron markings on the road which help separate traffic lanes
Hazard	Anything that could be a source of danger on the road
Intoxicant	Something that can affect a person's behaviour, perception, mood or alertness
Invalid-carriages	Vehicles specially designed or constructed for people with disabilities. This does not apply to conventional motor cars which are specially adapted for disabled persons and which are permitted to use a motorway
National road	A major road linking urban areas and consisting of motorway roads identified by 'M' route numbers, for example M1, and other routes identified by 'N' route numbers, for example N11
Land tractor	Commonly called 'an agricultural tractor', these vehicles are designed to work on land in connection with agricultural, forestry or land drainage-type operations and are driven on a public road only when proceeding to or from the site of such work
Lighting-up hours	The period commencing one half-hour after sunset on any day and expiring one half-hour before sunrise on the next day.
Luas	The tram system operating in Dublin city and suburbs
Manoeuvre	Any action to steer or change the course of a vehicle, such as moving off, changing lanes, leaving a roundabout, turning left or right, taking U-turns or reversing
Median space	A gap provided in the centre of a dual carriageway to allow vehicles to cross through or turn onto another road

Merging	Coming together. For example, traffic entering a motorway from a slip road and joining other traffic
Moped	A light motorcycle of 50cc or less that has a maximum speed of 45km/h
Motorcycle engine capacity	Cubic capacity or CC of engine
Motorcycle power rating	Engine power output
Muscular atrophy	Wasting of muscles
Nearside	Left-hand side
Negligence	Failing to act with reasonable care
Night-driving mode (mirror)	Darkened reflection which reduces dazzle
Non-national road	A local or regional road linking villages and towns within a county or district identified by an R or L number sign
Offside	Right-hand side
Ophthalmic optician	An optician qualified to prescribe glasses and contact lenses and detect eye diseases
Outer lane	The lane nearest the centre of the road in a dual carriageway or two- or three-lane motorway
Permit	A legal document giving permission to do something like park in a particular place or use certain roads
Pinch points	Traffic calming measure where sections of the road are narrowed to reduce speed
Pointsman	A Garda who controls the flow of traffic
Prescription	A written note from a doctor or hospital stating what medicines a person should take and when they should take them
Professional drivers	Drivers whose main income is from driving, such as bus, coach and haulage drivers
Radial tyres (radial ply tyres)	Tyres with cords made of steel and other materials, which run around under the treads to strengthen them and make them last longer
Retarder	A device that reduces the speed of the vehicle without using the brakes
Safe headway	A safe distance between two vehicles on the road
'Sam Browne'	A wide strap, made of reflective material, worn around the waist with a strap diagonally over the right shoulder
Secondary controls	Devices in a vehicle that do not direct its movement or braking but control how the driver sees out of the vehicle and how the vehicle is seen; examples are de-misters, windscreen wipers, washers and hazard lights

Single lane (for shuttle working)	Control of traffic through road works one-way system where manual operated stop/go signs are in use
Stationary	Stopped, for example in a line of traffic, at a stop light or in a parking space
Swan neck	The course followed by a vehicle when the driver passes the correct point for taking a right turn and needs to make a bigger effort to correct the position when completing the turn
Tabard	Sleeveless yellow fluorescent vest worn by motorcyclists with 'L' plates clearly displayed to front and rear.
Tachograph	A device that measures and records the speed, distance and time travelled by a vehicle
Tailgating	Driving too close to a vehicle in front
Tarpaulin	Waterproof canvas material used to cover cargo being transported
T-junction	A junction where the meeting of a minor road with a major road forms a 'T' shape
Tread (tyres)	The grooves on a tyre which provide a grip on the road
Variable message sign	An upright electronic sign, whose content changes to inform on roads and road safety
Vigilant	Careful, watchful, looking out for possible danger
Work vehicles	Vehicles used at sites or roadworks that usually do not drive on the road
Yield	Give way to other road users

Index

///